ROUTLEDGE LIBRARY EDITIONS:
CURRICULUM

Volume 3

THE IMPACT OF THE NATIONAL CURRICULUM ON THE TEACHING OF FIVE-YEAR-OLDS

THE IMPACT OF THE NATIONAL CURRICULUM ON THE TEACHING OF FIVE-YEAR-OLDS

THEO COX AND SUSAN SANDERS

LONDON AND NEW YORK

First published in 1994 by Falmer

This edition first published in 2019
by Routledge
2 Park Square, Milton Park, Abingdon, Oxon OX14 4RN

and by Routledge
711 Third Avenue, New York, NY 10017

Routledge is an imprint of the Taylor & Francis Group, an informa business

© 1994 T. Cox and S. Sanders

All rights reserved. No part of this book may be reprinted or reproduced or utilised in any form or by any electronic, mechanical, or other means, now known or hereafter invented, including photocopying and recording, or in any information storage or retrieval system, without permission in writing from the publishers.

Trademark notice: Product or corporate names may be trademarks or registered trademarks, and are used only for identification and explanation without intent to infringe.

British Library Cataloguing in Publication Data
A catalogue record for this book is available from the British Library

ISBN: 978-1-138-31956-1 (Set)
ISBN: 978-0-429-45387-8 (Set) (ebk)
ISBN: 978-1-138-31828-1 (Volume 3) (hbk)
ISBN: 978-1-138-32149-6 (Volume 3) (pbk)
ISBN: 978-0-429-45470-7 (Volume 3) (ebk)

Publisher's Note
The publisher has gone to great lengths to ensure the quality of this reprint but points out that some imperfections in the original copies may be apparent.

Disclaimer
The publisher has made every effort to trace copyright holders and would welcome correspondence from those they have been unable to trace.

The Impact of the National Curriculum on the Teaching of Five-Year-Olds

Theo Cox and Susan Sanders

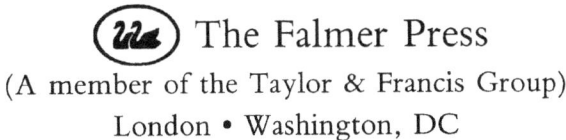

The Falmer Press
(A member of the Taylor & Francis Group)
London • Washington, DC

UK	The Falmer Press, 4 John Street, London WC1N 2ET
USA	The Falmer Press, Taylor & Francis Inc., 1900 Frost Road, Suite 101, Bristol, PA 19007

© T. Cox and S. Sanders 1994

All rights reserved. No part of this publication may be reproduced, stored in a retrieval system, or transmitted in any form or by any means, electronic, mechanical, photocopying, recording or otherwise, without permission in writing from the Publisher.

First published in 1994

A catalogue record for this book is available from the British Library

Library of Congress Cataloging-in-Publication Data are available on request

ISBN 0 7507 0250 8 cased
ISBN 0 7507 0251 6 paper

Jacket design by Caroline Archer

Typeset in 12/14pt Bembo
Graphicraft Typesetters Ltd., Hong Kong

Printed in Great Britain by Burgess Science Press, Basingstoke on paper which has a specified pH value on final paper manufacture of not less than 7.5 and is therefore 'acid free'.

Contents

List of Tables and Figures		*vii*
Acknowledgments		*viii*
Chapter 1	Introduction: The National Curriculum and the 1988 Education Reform Act	1

Part I: The Study

Chapter 2	Aims and Conduct of the Research Study and Background Information on the Schools	12
Chapter 3	Preparing for the National Curriculum	28
Chapter 4	Teaching the National Curriculum	42
Chapter 5	Differentiating the National Curriculum	58
Chapter 6	The Teachers' Views on the Impact of the National Curriculum	76
Chapter 7	Teachers' Attitudes to the National Curriculum	101
Chapter 8	Summary, Discussion and Conclusions	114

Part II: Selected Issues Arising from the Study

Chapter 9	Pedagogical and Curricular Issues	132
Chapter 10	Slower Learners and Socially Disadvantaged Children	147
Chapter 11	Educating Children Under Five	166

Contents

Appendix 1	The Teachers' Attitude Scale	187
Appendix 2	Additional Tables and Figures	189
References		194
Name Index		203
Subject Index		205

List of Tables and Figures

Table 1	Roll size of sample schools	13
Table 2	School type	13
Table 3	Catchment areas of sample schools	14
Table 4	The sample of teachers	18
Table 5	The 'core sample' of teachers	19
Table 6	Regular support for the class teacher	25
Table 7	LEA INSET programme 1988–1982	31
Figure 1	Teachers' attitude scale scores in 1989	104
Figure 2	Teachers' attitude scale scores in 1990	105
Figure 3	Teachers' attitude scale scores in 1991	106
Table 8	Teachers' views on the National Curriculum over three years	110
Table A.1	Headteachers' and class teachers' mean attitude scale scores	190
Table A.2	Teachers' mean attitude scale scores over three years: Headteachers and class teachers combined	190
Figure A.1	'Core sample' teachers' attitude scale scores in 1989	191
Figure A.2	'Core sample' teachers' attitude scale scores in 1990	192
Figure A.3	'Core sample' teachers' attitude scale scores in 1991	193

Acknowledgments

The research study upon which this book is based was funded by the University of Wales Faculty of Eduction. The authors would like to thank the Director of Education of the LEA in which the study was carried out for his permission to carry out the study, and the county council officers who provided background information on the participating schools and on the county INSET programme concerning the National Curriculum. Our special thanks are due to the headteachers and Year 1 class teachers of the participating schools for their cooperation with the research project at a time when they were fully occupied in meeting the new demands of the National Curriculum and other changes stemming from the 1988 Education Reform Act.

In addition we wish to thank Richard Daugherty, former Chairman of the Curriculum Council for Wales, for his helpful advice concerning policy developments within the council, and for making available various Council publications. We also wish to thank Miss Frances Wood, Librarian of the University College of Swansea Department of Education Library, and her staff, for their helpfulness in locating and obtaining various publications. Our thanks are also due to members of staff in the Education Department of University College Swansea, namely: Alan Dobbins (Senior Lecturer), for his help in the data analysis; Alice Laing (Departmental Research Fellow) and Gill Harper Jones (Lecturer), for reading and commenting on Chapters 10 and 11 respectively; and Jackie Curry and Sian Davies for their secretarial assistance.

Finally, but by no means least, we record our thanks to Jane Evans, our Project Research Officer, for carrying out all of the teacher interviews.

Theo Cox
Susan Sanders
October 1993

Chapter 1

Introduction: The National Curriculum and the 1988 Education Reform Act

Since the 1944 Education Act, until the introduction of the National Curriculum primary teachers have enjoyed considerable freedom of educational thought and practice, and, in contrast to their secondary school colleagues, their work has not been constrained by the requirements of a national system of formal examinations. (The eleven-plus selection procedures did constrain the upper primary curriculum of some schools, it is true, but these procedures were largely abandoned in the 1960s.) Despite this enviable degree of autonomy, however, primary schools have been subject to a greater or lesser degree of control of their curriculum planning, teaching and classroom organization by the policies of their respective LEAs. At its best the influence of such policies has been of great benefit to primary schools in providing sound guidance and support, while respecting teachers' professional independence. However, such influence has been damaging in those cases where the strong advocacy of a particular LEA philosophy or approach to primary teaching has foisted upon teachers practices which they have neither understood fully nor accepted into their own thinking (see Alexander, 1992, for example).

The passing of the Education Reform Act (ERA) in 1988 marked a strikingly new phase in education characterized by central government control of the content of the curriculum across the 5 to 16 year age range. This was coupled with a deliberate weakening of the powers of local government in educational matters through the enforced delegation of their responsibilities for management and budgeting to the schools themselves. Chitty (1992) provides a lucid analysis of the political background to the introduction of this Act. His view of the Act is summed up in the following statement:

> It increased the powers of the Education Secretary to a quite alarming degree, and restored to central government a control over the school curriculum which had been surrendered in the inter-war period. While gathering more power to the centre, it simultaneously introduced important limitations on the functions of LEAs, who were forced to give greater autonomy to schools, heads and governing bodies. Above all, it effectively ended that ill defined partnership between central government, local government and individual schools which had been such a prominent feature of the educational scene since the settlement of 1944. (Chitty, 1992: 37)

However Chitty argues that the origin of the National Curriculum lay partly in Prime Minister James Callaghan's celebrated speech in October 1976 at Ruskin College, Oxford, which launched the 'great debate' in education. Amongst other things Callaghan advocated the need for a core curriculum of basic knowledge, greater teacher accountability, and the direct subordination of the secondary curriculum to the needs of the economy (for a collection of papers written to celebrate the tenth anniversary of that speech see Williams *et al.*, 1992).

As Chitty states, the major provisions of the 1988 Education Reform Act are:

1. the introduction of a National Curriculum for all state schools alongside a national system of assessment for pupils from 5 to 16 years. The Act defines mathematics, English and science as 'core subjects' (plus Welsh in Welsh medium schools in Wales), with a second group of 'foundation' subjects, namely: a modern foreign language (for secondary pupils only); Welsh as a second language for schools in Wales; technology; history; geography; art; music; and physical education.[1] Religious education was added later as a 'basic subject'.

Introduction

For most subjects the Act stated that there would be attainment targets for children aged 7, 11, 14 and 16, which would provide standards against which pupils' progress and performance could be assessed by the individual teacher and also, through a national system of tests (Standard Assessment Tasks or SATs). The detailed content of the National Curriculum, including the attainment targets, was laid down in subject orders (often referred to as 'National Curriculum folders' by teachers), supplemented by non-statutory programmes of study for each subject;

2 the introduction of a system of local management of schools (LMS) under which school budgets for staffing, premises and services were delegated from the LEA to individual schools;

3 the creation of a new tier of schooling comprising City Technology Colleges (CTCs) and grant maintained schools. The latter would choose to opt out of LEA control and receive direct funding from central government. The Act allowed the governors of all secondary schools and primary schools with over 300 registered pupils to apply to the Secretary of State for grant maintained status.

As enshrined in the ERA the content of the National Curriculum, although not its principle, has been the subject of considerable criticism (see, for example, Chitty, 1992; Lawton, 1988). Certainly, at the primary level, its strong subject orientation seems incompatible with the view of the curriculum expressed in the Plowden Report (Central Advisory Council for Education, England, 1967). This argues that the extent to which subject matter ought to be classified, and the headings under which such classifications are made will vary very much with the age of the children, with the demands made by the structure of the subject matter to be studied, and with the circumstances of the school. Pointedly the report states that 'Any practice which predetermines the pattern and imposes it upon all is to be condemmed' (para. 538). The report goes on to suggest that for young children the broadest division of the curriculum is suitable, e.g.

language, science, mathematics, environmental studies and the expressive arts. For older children (9 to 12) more subject divisions can be expected, although 'experience in secondary schools has shown that teaching of rigidly defined subjects, often by subject specialists, is far from suitable for the oldest children who will be in middle schools' (para. 538).

As recently as 1985 HMI proposed a curriculum model for children aged 5 to 16 which was based upon areas of learning and experience rather than traditional subjects, as follows:

> aesthetic and creative;
> human and social;
> linguistic and literary;
> mathematical;
> moral;
> physical;
> scientific;
> spiritual;
> technological. (DES, 1985, para. 33)

These areas were not suggested as discrete elements to be taught separately and in isolation from one another and were not equated with particular subjects, although it was acknowledged that some subjects would contribute more to some areas than others.

The National Curriculum guidance document entitled *A Framework for the Whole Curriculum 5–16 in Wales* (CCW, 1989) puts forward a list of eight 'elements of learning' which correspond closely to the areas of learning just listed. It is advocated that the discrete subjects of the National Curriculum should be subsumed within these elements which should facilitate planning on a cross-subject basis and 'help to break down a still prevalent tendency to develop the teaching of individual subjects in isolation from others' (CCW, 1989: 5). However, the fact remains that this document, together with an equivalent document published by the National Curriculum Council (1990) is for guidance only while the full legislative weight of the ERA is channelled through separate subject orders.

Despite the fact that it seems somewhat at odds with earlier, alternative curriculum models, the National Curriculum could still be said to represent a careful analysis of the knowledge, skills and understanding which children need to learn, albeit within a narrow subject framework. It does not prescribe *how* this content should be taught so that, at the primary level, for example, it should be possible to teach it through a thematic, topic approach to some extent. Indeed the guidance document produced by the Curriculum Council for Wales (CCW, 1989) states that the primary curriculum will be designed in an integrated manner and often implemented through topic or thematic work (but see Chapter 9 of this book on this question).

Further, it was not intended that the National Curriculum should constitute the whole of the primary or secondary school curriculum. Indeed the National Curriculum Council (NCC) argued that the National Curriculum alone could not provide the broad and balanced curriculum to which all pupils were entitled; it identified five broad themes which underpinned the curriculum, particularly at the secondary school level. These were: economic and industrial understanding, careers education and guidance, health education, education for citizenship, and environmental education (NCC, 1990). In addition, this NCC document stressed the importance of the dimensions of equal opportunities for all pupils and their preparation for life in a multicultural community as underpinning all teaching in schools.

In his recent interim report on the revision of the National Curriculum Sir Ron Dearing (NCC, 1993b)[2] proposes to increase the amount of teaching time available for discretionary use by the teacher. Such a move would clearly allow schools more scope to teach beyond the confines of the National Curriculum.

A central element of the National Curriculum was an elaborate system for the assessment of children's performance and progress. This was designed to provide both formative information, which would enable teachers to match the learning tasks more closely to individual's level of knowledge, skill and understanding, and summative information, which would provide a summary of a child's level of achievement in a given area of skill or knowledge. Formative assessment was to be carried out by the teacher using a self-designed or school-designed system, while summative assessment was to be carried out by means of nationally prescribed Standard Assessment Tasks (SATs). These were designed to reflect normal teaching practice as far as possible, and were to be given by the class teacher, but they were standardized in their method of administration and scoring and would yield results that were comparable from school to school. As such they could be used to provide overall pupil performance data for the national 'league tables' of school performance which were introduced by the 1988 Act.

This assessment system was based on the work of a Task Group on Assessment and Testing set up by the government under the leadership of Professor Paul Black. Their recommendations were contained in a main report (DES/Welsh Office, 1988a) and three supplementary reports (DES/Welsh Office, 1988b). The overseeing and subsequent development of the National Curriculum assessment system was entrusted to the School Examinations and Assessment Council (SEAC) set up by the government at the same time as the National Curriculum Council (NCC) in England and the Curriculum Council for Wales (CCW). (NCC and SEAC were merged into a new body called the School Curriculum and Assessment Authority on October 1st 1993, while the CCW is being replaced by a new Assessment and Curriculum Authority for Wales from April 1994.)

It could be argued that the time scale for the phased introduction of the National Curriculum and its associated apparatus for assessment was very tight in terms of allowing teachers sufficient time to adapt to each element as it came on stream. At Key Stage 1, for example, the full National Curriculum, comprising nine subjects, plus Welsh for schools in Wales, and religious education, was introduced during the period 1989 to 1993. However the demands placed upon the teachers at this key stage were significantly increased by a succession of changes to existing subject orders and assessment arrangements which took place during this period. One example is that the mathematics subject order was revised in 1991.

While these additional changes were likely to be very frustrating to hard pressed teachers trying to get to grips with the essentials of the National Curriculum it has to be said that, in some measure, these changes were made by the present government in response to concerted action by the teachers themselves. This was especially so in the case of the national assessment arrangements which are currently being streamlined.

Introduction

The recent *post hoc* changes to the National Curriculum have now culminated in a full scale review of the whole system which has been entrusted by the Education Secretary to Sir Ron Dearing, currently Chairman of the SEAC, and also to the Chairman of the Curriculum Council for Wales. The overall aim of the review is to achieve a slimming down of the National Curriculum and its assessment procedures but, in the course of conducting it, Dearing is raising a number of key issues upon which he is inviting the views of teachers in a commendably frank and consultative fashion (see his series of five articles in the *Times Educational Supplement* commencing 17 September 1993 (Dearing 1993 a, b, c, d, e)). He has already produced an interim report (NCC, 1993b) and is to make his final recommendations in December 1993. In one of these articles he states his view that teachers wished 'to take time to get things right and, meanwhile, put a brake on the rate of change' (Dearing, 1993a: 21). Accordingly he has recommended that no further curricular changes should be made before September 1995. He has made it clear that he is seeking to lighten and rationalize the present over-cluttered structure of the National Curriculum without going back to the drawing board. He is keen not to jettison those elements which teachers have worked so hard to implement to date.

Studying the Impact of the National Curriculum at Key Stage One

The aim of our research study, which was funded by the University of Wales, was to study the impact of the National Curriculum upon the teaching of 5-year-old children, i.e. those in Year 1 of this curriculum, as judged by the teachers themselves. We decided to focus upon this age group in particular since they were the very first to experience the National Curriculum. The study was conducted in a representative sample of the primary and infant schools of a South Wales LEA from 1989 to 1990, with a short follow-up study in 1991. The focus of the study was upon the National Curriculum as such but, inevitably, the responses of the teachers at interview were partly coloured by their perceptions of the effects of other innovations introduced by the ERA, including LMS.

The Impact of the National Curriculum

It is important to bear in mind that the study was carried out in Wales, which has its own independent body, the Curriculum Council for Wales (CCW). There are certain differences between the National Curriculum in Wales from that in England which, taken together, constitute a distinctive 'Welsh dimension'. The most important of these is the fact that, in Wales, the Welsh language is an additional core or non-core subject, depending on whether the school teaches through the medium of Welsh or English. The consequence of this, of course, is that the weight of the National Curriculum is greater in Wales than in England and the lack of fluency in Welsh of many primary school teachers in Wales poses some difficulty. In addition, four non-core subjects, namely history, geography, art and music, have been given separate orders, the result of which pupils in schools in Wales will follow somewhat different programmes of study from their peers in England.

The LEA within which the study was carried out had its own distinctive policies for primary education which were transmitted through its team of primary advisors and advisory teachers, and also through a series of policy documents published from 1987 onwards. The latter state the basic principles of that policy and their detailed application in the various areas of the primary curriculum. In addition the schools received all of the statutory and non-statutory National Curriculum guidance documents produced by the CCW.

Structure of the Book

Part I of this book starts with the essential background information on the schools, teachers and children in the study sample and details of the research questionnaires. This is followed by a detailed presentation of the study findings in Chapters 3 to 7. Chapter 8 provides a summary of the main findings, a discussion of them in the light of other National Curriculum studies and reports, and our conclusions.

In Part II we discuss in greater depth selected major issues arising from the study in the light of the wider literature. These are pedagogical and curricular issues (Chapter 9), the education

Introduction

of slower learning and socially disadvantaged pupils (Chapter 10) and the education of under-5s (Chapter 11).

Notes

1 Strictly speaking these subjects are described in the Act as 'non-core' subjects, since all of the subjects, including the 'core subjects', are foundation subjects. Throughout this book we have used the term non-core subjects, in line with correct usage. However, where teachers have used the term 'foundation subjects' (meaning non-core subjects) we have retained their wording.
2 Sir Ron Dearing's final report advising changes to the National Curriculum, School Curriculum and Assessment Authority, 1994 was published too late to be incorporated in detail in our book. However his recommendations regarding Key Stages 1 and 2 appear to be broadly in line with those in his interim report which are referred to in the following chapters. The only exception to this is the fact that the final report recommends that, at Key Stages 1–3, the National Curriculum should be slimmed down to free some 20 per cent of teaching time for use at the discretion of the school, whereas the interim report suggested a lower percentage of discretionary time at Key Stage 1 (10–15 per cent). (See Chapter 8, page 129).

Part I
The Study

Chapter 2

Aims and Conduct of the Research Study and Background Information on the Schools

Selection of Sample Schools

The study was carried out in a South Wales LEA which was predominantly urban in character but included some rural areas containing village communities. Our aim was to draw up a representative sample of the LEA's 142 primary and infant schools. This would be small enough to enable the team's research officer to carry out structured interviews with the headteachers and Year 1 class teachers. The first step was to obtain background information from the LEA on its primary and infant schools in terms of their roll size, type (infant or primary), catchment area, status (maintained or voluntary) and their linguistic medium of teaching (Welsh or English). Then, using a method of random selection, we drew a sample of twenty-eight schools, approximately one in five, which reflected the range of variation of the LEA's schools in terms of the features just described. Each of these schools was approached and if a headteacher felt unable to take part in the project, as a number of them did, owing to great pressure of work, an alternative, equivalent school was approached. Just before the commencement of the study, two schools from the group of twenty-eight withdrew, reducing the final sample to twenty-six schools (between one in five and one in six of the total number of schools). Background information on these schools now follows.

School size

Table 1 shows the distribution of school size in terms of number of pupils on roll. The cut-off points between the divisions of size

The Research Study and Background Information

Table 1   Roll size of sample schools

No. of pupils on roll	No. of schools
Small : 161 or fewer	9
Medium: 162–250	9
Large : 251–400	8
Total	26

Table 2   School type

Type	No. of schools
LEA Infant	4 (20)
LEA Primary	19 (102)
LEA Welsh-medium (Primary)	1 (10)
Voluntary Aided	2 (10)

Note: The numbers in brackets refer to the LEA's primary/infant schools as a whole.

were obtained by ordering the sizes of all 142 of the LEA's schools and then marking off equal thirds.

Type of School

Table 2 shows the distribution of schools in terms of their type, with the numbers of equivalent schools throughout the LEA in brackets for comparison.

It will be seen from Table 2 that the LEA Welsh-medium primary schools were slightly underrepresented in our sample. Otherwise the distribution of schools seems satisfactory.

Catchment Area

With the aim of obtaining a representative spread of sample schools in terms of their type of catchment area, the LEA was asked to indicate, for each of its schools, whether it served a mainly middle-class, a skilled working-class or lower working-class area. On the basis of this information the sample of twenty-eight schools (subsequently twenty-six) was drawn up so as to reflect the distribution of types of catchment found in the LEA

Table 3 Catchment areas of sample schools

Type of area	No. of schools
Mixed middle-class/skilled working-class	17 (113)
Skilled working-class/lower working-class (i.e. semi or unskilled or unemployed)	9 (29)
Total	26 (142)

Note: The figures in brackets refer to the LEA's primary/infant schools as a whole.

schools overall. It should be stressed that the LEA information was based upon the professional knowledge of a senior officer who knew the schools well.

Once the final sample of schools had been selected the headteachers were asked to indicate the nature of their school catchment areas in the same terms as those described above. In the event some of them found difficulty making an objective judgment of the social composition of their areas and it was therefore decided to use a cruder classification as shown in Table 3.

Table 3 shows that the distribution of sample schools in terms of their catchment areas was reasonably representative of that in the LEA as a whole but perhaps with a slight overweighting of schools serving 'lower working-class' catchments. However, given the subjective nature of this information the figures in the table should be regarded with caution. Of the nine schools serving predominantly lower working-class areas five had been designated by the LEA as 'social priority area' schools before that practice was discontinued.

Research Procedure: Aim and Method

The primary aim of the study was to obtain the views of a representative sample of primary headteachers and Year 1 class teachers in the chosen LEA on the impact of the National Curriculum upon the education of 5-year-old children. To achieve this aim we judged that the use of structured interviews, based upon questionnaires, would be the most appropriate research technique. The use of a postal questionnaire would have allowed us access to a much bigger sample but this would have limited the scope of the types of question that we could ask and, more importantly, would have precluded the possibility of probing and elaborating the teachers' initial responses to questions (Oppenheim, 1992). Limited project resources precluded the use of direct observation of teachers and children working in their classrooms, desirable as that would have been as a complementary technique to that of interviewing the teachers. The research team comprised the two co-authors and a part-time research officer who was an experienced primary teacher.

The First Round of Interviews

Separate questionnaires were drawn up for the headteachers and Year 1 class teachers respectively. Year 1 teachers were defined as teachers of all infant classes containing children eligible for Year 1 of the National Curriculum, i.e. between 5 and 6 years of age.

The headteachers' questionnaire (1989) covered the following topics:

  the school and its background;
  organization and staffing;
  home–school links;
  children with special needs/learning difficulties (identification and provision);
  curriculum planning prior to the National Curriculum (including assessment and record keeping;
  preparing for the National Curriculum (curriculum development and INSET);
  anticipated problems in delivering the National Curriculum and its anticipated effects on the teaching of the core subjects and on the teaching of children with special needs;
  support and resources needed.

The class teacher's questionnaire (1989) covered the following topics:

  class composition, classroom organization and staffing;
  curriculum and teaching methods (including assessment and record keeping and the use of free play);

curriculum development and INSET (preparation for teaching the National Curriculum);

anticipated effects of the National Curriculum on the teaching of core subjects and on teaching children with special needs;

anticipated problems in teaching the National Curriculum;

support and resources needed.

In addition to the above questions the questionnaires included a short fourteen-item scale designed to measure teachers' attitudes to the National Curriculum to be completed in writing by the teachers themselves (see Appendix 1). This yielded an overall attitude score but the teachers' responses to each item could also be analysed separately (see Chapter 7 for further details).

Prior to their use in the study both questionnaires were piloted on a small sample of headteachers and class teachers from another LEA. As a result of this exercise some of the original questions were eliminated or rephrased to make them clearer. In addition it was suggested by the pilot sample teachers themselves that, in order to cut down on valuable interview time, the more factual questions could be completed by the teachers before the interview. In accordance with this suggestion the questionnaires were circulated to the sample teachers about two weeks in advance of their interviews with a request for them to complete specified questions in writing beforehand.

The first round of interviewing took place during the summer term of 1989, i.e. the term immediately preceding the introduction of the National Curriculum at Key Stage 1 in September 1989. (A few interviews had to be postponed until the following term.) On average each interview lasted about an hour for headteachers and three-quarters of an hour for class teachers.

The Second Round of Interviews

The second round of interviews took place approximately one year after the first round, during the summer term of 1990, i.e. toward the end of the first year of the implementation of the National Curriculum. The interview questionnaires were closely

The Research Study and Background Information

related to those used in the first round, suitably adapted to take account of the fact that the National Curriculum had been in operation for nearly one year.

The headings of the headteachers' questionnaire were as follows:

> general information (updating that obtained in 1989);
> children with special needs/learning difficulties (identification and provision);
> curriculum planning and INSET under the National Curriculum (including assessment and record keeping);
> effects of the National Curriculum on:
> > curriculum, organization and teaching of the four core subjects,
> > thematic, cross-curricular work,
> > teaching children with special needs and under-5s;
> views on the impact of the National Curriculum:
> > preparedness for teaching the National Curriculum,
> > problems and difficulties experienced,
> > benefits and disadvantages of the National Curriculum,
> > further support and resources needed.

The headings for the class teachers' questionnaire were as follows:

> class composition, classroom organization and staffing;
> curriculum and teaching methods (including assessment and record keeping and the use of free play);
> curriculum development and INSET under the National Curriculum;
> effects of the National Curriculum on:
> > curriculum, organization and teaching of the core subjects,
> > teaching children with special needs and the under-5s;
> views on the impact of the National Curriculum:
> > preparedness for teaching the National Curriculum,
> > problems and difficulties experienced,
> > benefits and disadvantages of the National Curriculum,
> > further support and resources needed.

Table 4 The sample of teachers

	Headteachers	Class teachers	Total
1989 (lst interviews)	26	31	57
1990 (2nd interviews)	24	34	58
1991 (follow-up)	21	31	52

The two sets of questionnaires covering the first year of implementation of the National Curriculum comprised the main body of data for the study. However, during the following year (1990–91) it was decided to ask the participating schools if they would be willing to complete short written follow-up questionnaires concerning the impact of the National Curriculum and their views on it. Nearly all of the schools agreed to do so and the follow-up questionnaires were therefore sent to the participating schools for completion by the headteachers and Year 1 class teachers respectively in the summer term 1991. Each questionnaire (headteachers' and class teachers') contained selected questions from the questionnaires used for the second round of interviews in 1990 plus the short attitude scale. In this way the scope of the study was extended by a further year.

The Sample of Teachers

Table 4 shows the size of the teacher sample for the first and second round of interviews and also for the administration of the written follow-up questionnaire. The questionnaires were completed by the headteachers in the sample schools and the teachers of all infant classes which contained some Year 1 children.

As might be expected there was some turnover in the composition of the class teacher sample over the three occasions on which data were gathered, due to staffing changes within the schools. In contrast the composition of the headteachers sample remained virtually unchanged over the period, apart from five withdrawals from the study owing to pressure of work or retirement. Table 5 shows the extent to which the same teachers were involved in two or more years of the study. These teachers can be thought of as comprising a 'core sample' although they are

Table 5 The 'core sample' of teachers

	Headteachers	Class teachers	Total
Present in 1989/1990	24	26	50
Present in 1989/1990/1991	21	14	35

only separated out in the analyses of the attitude scale data (see Chapter 7).

A comparison of Tables 4 and 5 shows that the majority of headteachers and class teachers who took part in the first round of interviews in 1989 were also present for the second round of interviews in 1990 but, by 1991, just under half of the original sample of class teachers were still present in the study.

Background Information on the Sample Schools

Background information on the sample schools was provided by the headteachers in the first interview questionnaire completed at the outset of the study. This was updated, where appropriate, in the second interview questionnaire completed in 1990. In addition some information about home–school links was provided by the class teachers in their questionnaires.

General information
Of the twenty-six schools four operated on the 'open plan' system with free access between open teaching areas. Twenty-one schools had nursery classes attached to them which were mostly attended by 3 to 4-year-old children on a half-time basis. In the smallest schools four of the headteachers had full teaching responsibility for a class although they received some teaching support to enable them to carry out their headship duties. Of the remaining twenty-two headteachers twelve stated that they regularly engaged in some form of teaching (ten in 1990).

The status of Welsh in the schools
In twenty-two of the twenty-six schools Welsh was a non-core subject in the National Curriculum. In the remaining four schools it was a core subject which meant that the children attending

these schools would be tested in Welsh rather than English at the end of Key Stage 1. Of the latter schools one was a designated Welsh-medium school while the remainder used a combination of English and Welsh for teaching purposes.

Classroom Organization and Staffing

Regarding the location of the Year 1 children, in seventeen classes they were taught in single age group 'I1' classes for 5 to 6-year-olds. In the remaining thirteen classes they were taught in combination with one or more other age groups. (Information was missing for one class teacher.)

In 1989 only eight of the headteachers reported that their infant teachers engaged in any form of team teaching and nine in 1990. This mainly appeared to take the form of combining classes for certain practical activities such as music and drama, but also Welsh, in order to capitalize upon the expertise of particular members of staff.

Of the twenty-two primary schools, eleven had a teacher with designated responsibility for the infants department but the remainder did not and this situation did not change in 1990. Four of the headteachers stated that the curriculum for infant children was planned separately from that for juniors but, by 1990, this number had dropped to two.

On the question of pattern of infant classroom organization the majority of headteachers stated either that they recommended a pattern to the class teacher, e.g. an 'integrated day', but left the final choice to her or him, or they expected the infant teacher to decide on their own preferred pattern.

In 1989 nearly half of the primary head teachers (ten) claimed that the pattern of infant classroom organization was different from that in the junior department, referring to such features as their greater informality and their more practical, play based approach. Other differences mentioned were the use of the integrated day pattern of organization in infant classes and the fact that in some cases they contained mixed age groups. However, by 1990 the number of schools where the pattern of classroom organization was described as different had dropped to five. This

The Research Study and Background Information

could possibly be a reflection of academic and other pressures exerted upon the schools' infant departments but this is speculative.

Children with Special Needs and Learning Difficulties

In 1989 nine headteachers reported having one or more children in their infant departments with statements of special need, with most of the classes involved having only one such pupil. One headteacher commented that the policy of the LEA seemed to be not to issue formal statements in respect of children under 7.[1] In 1990 there were six statemented children at the infant stage but eleven headteachers stated that they were planning to refer particular children with a view to their being statemented. Again it is possible that this reflected a change in the educational climate in some schools following the introduction of the National Curriculum and other changes stemming from the ERA.

Regarding school procedures for the early detection of children's learning difficulties seventeen headteachers reported that these were based upon teacher observation and discussion with other staff, including the headteacher, and eleven headteachers mentioned discussion with or referral to the district educational psychologist. Only six headteachers mentioned specifically that any cases of learning difficulty would be discussed with the parents, although this does not necessarily mean that the other headteachers would not have done so.

By the the following year (1990) the detection procedures appeared to have changed very little but one headteacher reported the appointment of a member of staff as a coordinator for special needs who would prepare a written policy document on the school's provision for special needs. (Hitherto very few primary schools within this LEA appeared to have made such appointments but this situation was beginning to change with the appointment of a new county adviser for special needs.) In 1989 only two headteachers reported that their schools had produced written guidelines on their policies concerning children's special needs and in 1990 this number had increased by one with another two headteachers stating their intention of producing them.

The children in the sample schools with statements of

special educational need would, of course have received special provision and support as of right. On the question of support for non-statemented children with learning difficulties, twenty-one headteachers reported that some form of support teaching was available in addition to any extra help that the class teacher managed to offer. The support teachers typically worked with small groups of children with learning difficulties, either within the children's classrooms or by withdrawing them or by a combination of these arrangements.

Parental Involvement

The headteachers were asked whether parents were encouraged by the school to help in the education of their children and, if so, in what ways. As might be expected all of them stated that they encouraged parental involvement, particularly in the area of children's reading and language skills. In addition some schools set the children homework (but not necessarily for infant pupils) and encouraged the parents to support their children in doing this. Many of the schools were operating within a LEA organized scheme aimed at directly involving parents in the development of their children's reading skills. Under this scheme, known as 'Children and Parents Enjoy Reading' (CAPER), the LEA provided the participating schools with attractive reading books for the children to take home to read with their parents on a regular basis. In addition it provided advisory support for schools taking part in the scheme. (See also Chapter 11.)

The headteachers were also asked if parents assisted directly in the work of the school. Well over half of them (fifteen) reported that they did so and another three headteachers planned for their parents to do so. Parental contributions included assistance in the school library, accompanying children on school trips and assistance in practical curricular activities such as cooking, art and craft. Only five headteachers mentioned any parental involvement in the teaching of the core subjects, such as listening to children reading or assisting in science work.

The class teachers were also asked whether the parents were involved in the teaching of the core subjects either at home or at school. The majority of teachers reported that the parents listened to their children reading at home, although with varying frequency. A few teachers mentioned some problems in this respect such as the non-return of school reading books loaned by the school to the parents, or lack of parental interest in such involvement despite the school's encouragement.

In reply to a question concerning the parents' direct involvement in the teaching of core subjects at school twenty teachers indicated that parents were not involved, although some parents assisted in non-core classroom activities such as art or cookery. Only six teachers stated that parents were involved directly in children's core curricular activities. Their involvement ranged from listening to children reading; assisting the teacher in maths or reading; helping in the teaching of Welsh (Welsh speaking parents); and supporting a specific core subject activity if requested by the teacher.

In summary all of the schools claimed to have a policy of encouraging parents to be actively involved in the development of their children's reading skills at home but parental assistance within the school, when it occurred, appeared to be confined to non-core curricular activities in all but a few schools.

The Sample Teachers and Their Classes

The following information on the Year 1 infant classes was provided by the teachers through the questionnaires which they completed in 1989 and 1990.

Class size and age range
In 1989 the majority of the teachers (twenty-one) reported class sizes of between twenty and thirty pupils, with seven having smaller classes and three having larger classes. The distribution was similar in 1990. Regarding age range, over half of the teachers (seventeen) had classes containing only Year 1 children, i.e. 5 to 6-year-olds; seven had classes of 4 to 6-year-olds (i.e. Reception and Year 1 children); three had classes of 5 to 7-year-olds, and three had classes of 4 to 7-year-olds. (Information was missing for one teacher in the sample.) The distribution was similar in 1990.

The Impact of the National Curriculum

The majority of classes (twenty-six in both 1989 and 1990) consisted solely of children whose first language was English and only five classes (six in 1990) contained some children with a different mother tongue. (Half of the latter children were Welsh-speaking and the remainder spoke one of a range of languages from Europe, the Middle East or the Indian subcontinent.)

Range of children's abilities

The teachers were asked to indicate the range of abilities shown by their children in respect of mathematics and language. In both subjects the range was very wide. For example, in English, children's levels of reading ranged from the recognition of just a few words to reading fluently with good comprehension. In mathematics (number) the range covered little or no recognition of written number to competence in addition and subtraction to 20, or even 100. The skill range would no doubt be wider in those classes with a wider age range.

Children with special needs

In 1989 five teachers reported having a child in their class with a statement of special need but there appeared to be only one such case in 1990. However a much larger number of teachers in both years claimed to have children in their classes with suspected special educational needs (nineteen teachers in 1989 and twenty-two teachers in 1990). The main problems associated with such needs were speech and language or reading difficulties, generally slow progress, difficulties in vision or hearing, or behaviour difficulties, sometimes linked with social immaturity.

Method of classroom organization

The teachers were asked to indicate which of the three following patterns of organizing classroom activities they used:

> *Pattern 1*: Whole class engaged in the same curriculum activity (maths, language, etc.) at the same time, whether working in groups or individually, and switched to another common activity at the teacher's direction;
> *Pattern 2*: Class divided into fixed groups and each group worked on a different curriculum activity from other

Table 6 Regular support for the class teacher

Type of support	1989 (N=31)	1990 (N=34)
None	5	10
Qualified helper (e.g. nursery nurse)	9	10
Unqualified helper (e.g. parent)	7	6
Other teacher (e.g. support teacher)	10	12
Student teacher	1	2
Secondary school pupil	10	7

groups (e.g. one group worked on maths, another on writing, etc.);

Pattern 3: Individual decisions were made on each activity time, either by the child or the teacher as to which particular activity the child will engage in.

In 1989 four teachers used Pattern 1, seven used Pattern 2 and the remaining teachers used a combination of the above patterns. One teacher, for example, stated that the whole class might be engaged in the same curriculum activity which might then be followed by 'integrated groups'. A similar distribution emerged in 1990 except that only one teacher claimed to be using Pattern 1 and one teacher used Pattern 3.

Teacher support
The teachers were asked what regular forms of classroom support they received. Their responses are summarized in Table 6.

The total numbers in Table 6 exceed the total number of teachers since each teacher might record more than one form of support. It will be noted that the number of teachers apparently without a regular form of classroom support was five in 1989 and ten in 1990.

Team teaching
The teachers were asked if they engaged in any form of team teaching or shared teaching. In 1989 ten teachers reported that they did and this number rose to sixteen in 1990. The forms of collaboration ranged from the complete sharing of combined classes by two or more teachers, to lesson sharing with other

teachers for the more specialized subjects such as music or physical education. In addition, some teachers referred to their collaboration with other teachers in curriculum planning and organization, including the planning of cross-curricular topics.

Note

1 This may have been due to pressures of work on the LEA's team of educational psychologists. The LEA carried out an annual screening survey of the basic attainments of all 7-year-old children in order to identify those with possible special needs/learning difficulties.

Summary

The Schools

On the basis of the objective data provided in this chapter we consider that our sample of schools was representative of the infant and primary schools within this particular LEA with regard to their size (number of pupils on roll), type (infant or primary, voluntary or state maintained), and type of social catchment area. The schools ranged in size from small village schools, where Year 1 pupils were taught in classes containing two or even three age groups, to large urban schools with single age group classes. Amongst the smaller schools were some where the headteacher had teaching responsibility for a class. Nearly all of the schools in the sample had a nursery class or classes attached to them.

The Classes

Most of the classes taught by the Year 1 teachers in the sample contained between twenty and thirty children. Their age ranged from four to seven years but over half of the classes contained only Year 1 children (five to six-year-olds). The range of the children's attainments in the basic skills was wide: at one extreme there were children with virtually no formal attainments in reading writing or number, and at the other, there were children whose attainments were well above average for their age. Although only a handful of children had formal statements of special educational need well over half of the teachers in the sample judged that their classes contained children with some form of special need with regard to their academic progress, general development or behaviour.

The majority of teachers appeared to use some form of 'integrated day' pattern of classroom organization, i.e., where groups of children work concurrently on different curricular activities, as well as other patterns of organization at certain times. Most teachers received some form of classroom assistance but less than one-third received help from a qualified worker. Between one-half and one-third of teachers engaged in some form of team teaching.

The Research Enquiry

The research procedure was based upon structured personal interviews carried out with the headteachers and Year 1 class teachers during the summer term immediately preceding the introduction of the National Curriculum at Key Stage 1 in September 1989. The teachers were reinterviewed approximately one year later, in the summer of 1990. In addition a short follow-up enquiry was carried out in the summer of 1991 by means of a written questionnaire. On the basis of these interviews the teachers' predictions of the impact of the National Curriculum on a variety of aspects of the schools' curricula, methods of classroom organization, teaching and assessment could be compared with their subsequent judgments of its actual impact. Also the nature and content of the INSET received by the teachers, or considered to be needed by them, could be compared before and after the introduction of the National Curriculum, as well as their needs for staffing and resourcing. Finally, changes in the teachers' general attitudes to the National Curriculum, and their views towards particular aspects of it could be compared over the period of the study. The results from all of these comparisons are presented in the next five chapters.

Chapter 3

Preparing for the National Curriculum

Introduction

In the past new curriculum initiatives have, in the main, come through the development of materials for classroom use, e.g. the development of software for mathematics by the SMILE project[1] or the coming together of enthusiastic teachers to disseminate 'good practice', e.g. the area groups run under the auspices of the Nuffield Mathematics Trust. In the secondary schools changes have also been driven by new examination syllabuses, of which the General Certificate of Secondary Education (GCSE) is a recent example. With the introduction of the National Curriculum, perhaps for the first time, changes were now to be driven by legislation. What should or could be provided to ensure that the legislation would be translated into classroom practice?

The rhetoric prior to the introduction of the National Curriculum emphasized the autonomy of the teacher to decide *how* to teach the content that would be laid down by it. It would have been incongruous for materials to have been developed centrally since the politics of privatization and insistence on market driven competition prevalent in government at that time would not had sat comfortably with the provision of official classroom materials. (Work on assessment was put out to tender, which might have been an option for curriculum materials too.) Publishers were extremely quick to produce textbooks and materials supposedly in line with National Curriculum directives, although on closer scrutiny, the early revisions appeared to have been in the main new covers and new publicity.

What fitted with the notion of the autonomous teacher was the notion of 'empowering' INSET in which the teachers' professional knowledge was valued, developed and shared with others. The 'cascade' model that had been tried and found varying success with the Technical and Vocational Education Initiative (TVEI) and with GCSE was used again in many local education authorities (LEAs). Curriculum 'specialists' attended INSET of varying lengths and returned to school to lead the implementation of the National Curriculum. HMI (DES, 1991: 10) appraising this INSET subsequently reported that 'Too little attention was given to training key people to be trainers of others.' The time scale of the production, the various subject documents and the costs of such INSET were obviously strong factors in the LEA's prioritization. Some subjects were familiar in the curriculum and also within typical LEA advisory support structures. Mathematics for example had received substantial funding in the post-Cockcroft days of the mid-1980s; others traditionally received less support, such as Welsh in non-traditionally Welsh-speaking areas or little support in the primary phase, such as Technology. Existing support structures and lead time in setting up new structures and new costs would be factors in the prioritization of LEA INSET programmes.

However the National Curriculum was not just about content. The second main prong, and to some extent the fundamental new element that was pedagogically difficult for teachers of younger pupils, was the notion of formalized and reported assessment procedures. Not only would the pupils be judged, but the politicians spoke of weeding out weak teachers and of parental choice as a result of league tables, leading to the running down of 'below standard' schools.

Satisfied that they were not going to be told *how* to teach and that the *what* would not necessarily be vastly different from current work, teachers' anxieties clustered around the assessment procedures (details of our findings appear in the next chapter). The preparation of teachers would need to allay these fears if only to contain the ground swell of resistance to the formal testing of 7-year-olds that followed the announcements.

The LEA Programme

Despite the fact that the next few years were to see the erosion of the powers of LEAs by the government, the onus of the preparation for the National Curriculum fell on them. Some provision was made centrally, for example, by those commissioned to produce assessment materials but with the purpose that 'trained' LEA representatives would do the subsequent work within the locality. Provision was split between assessment and individual subjects. Table 7 gives a brief description of the INSET programme devised by the LEA from which our research sample of schools was drawn.

Individual school programmes
In addition to the LEA-run INSET and the subsequent cascade, many schools used non-contact time to work on the implementation of the National Curriculum. Often these sessions were run totally in-house but from time to time there would be input from an outside agency such as the local university or higher education institution.

Written guidance
In addition to the INSET programme indicated above, schools also had access to a wide range of written materials. These varied from those produced centrally in England (DES) and those produced in Wales (CCW, Welsh Office) to those produced by the LEA and in some instances, those produced in-house by the school or cluster of schools.

An LEA Rationale

One of the LEA primary advisors, with particular responsibility for early years' education, was interviewed in a mostly non-structured way to unpick the LEA thinking behind the programme of INSET that was provided between 1988 and 1992. She was interviewed in 1989, 1990 and 1991. Documentation was also collected from the LEA.

The LEA had produced a series of policy statements that covered both the teaching of individual subjects and the ideology of primary school teaching in the eighteen months prior to 1989. With the arrival of the National Curriculum the LEA view was that 'the National Curriculum should fit in with the LEA policy

Table 7 LEA INSET programme 1988–1992

1988–1989

* Seminars for headteachers. 35 headteachers per day.

* Spring Term: Core subjects 2 representatives per school. Curriculum specialist and one other. 1 had to be an infant teacher. 2 days per subject.

* Headteachers' conference focussing on Thematic approaches.

1989–1990

* Programme informed by information gathered by visits by advisory team to every school in the LEA. Focus on assessment. 20 Headteachers are seconded part time in Autumn Term to develop INSET for Spring Term.

* Spring Term: Teaching of core subjects to rising 5-year olds. 2 by 1 workshops for 75 teachers (total 150).

1990–1991

* National Curriculum Assessment for all primary school teachers.
  3 by 1 days during Autumn and Spring Terms. Topics: Teacher Assessment, Record Keeping, Standard Assessment Tasks.

* Design and Technology. 2 teachers from each school. 3 by 1 days.

* History and geography. 2 teachers from each school. 2 by 1 days.

* Welsh

* Headteachers' meetings. Schools grouped by LEA into clusters. Meetings led by a primary advisor.

1991–1992

* Sessions for music, art and PE. 2 teachers from each school.

* Number of staff development days increased from 3 to 6 because of need for training in use of SATs and teacher assessment.

and not the other way round!' The cascade model was to be used. There was a commitment to continuity and progression with staff development days on the LEA documents being run jointly for primary and secondary schools. The message from the LEA to the schools, was 'It is not going to be right at the start — it will be a question of trial and error and we will all learn and benefit from hindsight and experience.'

The Effectiveness of the Support

The purpose of the INSET programmes was to prepare the teachers and the schools for the smoothest implementation of the National Curriculum possible. In order to consider how successful this programme was, headteachers and class teachers in our research sample were asked questions about the preparation they received and how prepared they felt as a result.

The success of the programmes is evaluated in terms of how the teachers felt rather than how they performed. Neither is it evaluated in terms of the teachers' comments about individual courses or tutors. The outcomes of the INSET concern us here.

The Headteachers' Views

In 1989 the headteachers were asked how well prepared they thought they and their staff were for the introduction of the National Curriculum for 5-year-olds in the next September. Under one-third felt well prepared. The large majority, nearly three-quarters, felt fairly well prepared and only one respondent felt poorly prepared. Whether this was due to good INSET provision or blissful ignorance remained to be seen.

> There is much enthusiasm on the part of staff which is tinged with apprehension!

Reasons for feeling well prepared included a notion of 'it's only what we are doing anyway'.

> School is already running along the lines required by the National Curriculum.
>
> Our last seven years have been good preparation!
>
> Our existing methodology and approach is comparable to that which will be required.
>
> We have tried to prepare ourselves over the past two years with the information available to us.
>
> In the main it's an extension of the practice which should be going on.

There were also strong indications of being overwhelmed with material from all sources. The LEA produced materials, while considered to be of good quality, added to this feeling.

> The cascade of material from DES, LEA and other advisory/statutory bodies is overwhelming.
>
> Not enough time has been given to absorb, assimilate and evaluate.
>
> What is due to come in may make all [our] planning out of date. [It's been] too much too quickly.

There was also a feeling that the issues concerning infant education had not really been tackled. This was not an uncommon feeling amongst teachers of younger pupils. They often reported that their area was overlooked.

> Not enough time has been given to developing the infant element in the curriculum.
>
> There has been little opportunity for infant teachers to get together to discuss problems.

The special problems of a small school were also highlighted.

> [All] the work has to be spread between three people and this puts extra pressure on them.

The Impact of the National Curriculum

By 1990 the headteachers were reporting a shift in confidence. Whereas three-quarters had felt only fairly well prepared now nearly one-half said they were well prepared, with the rest feeling fairly well prepared.

One headteacher reported that

> The staff are moving slowly along the path. Change cannot be enforced — it has to happen gently. [It is a] gradual process to build up to the National Curriculum.

Another headteacher reported that the staff now had a greater awareness and familiarity with the documents and was therefore able to put them into perspective a little, and that this had helped with future planning

In 1991 confidence dropped with only one-third of headteachers reporting that they were well prepared for the next year. Two-thirds reported feeling fairly well prepared commenting in particular on the proposed further changes to the mathematics and science orders.

Headteachers were also asked what additional INSET they felt was necessary both for themselves and for the class teachers. This gives us an indication of their notions of readiness. There was a wide range of needs suggested with many headteachers citing unique needs. However nearly half the headteachers mentioned training in assessment and record keeping for both themselves and their teachers.

How true a picture did the headteachers have of their schools' readiness and needs? We next looked at how the class teachers felt about their own preparation.

The Teachers' Views

The class teachers questioned in 1989 had similar feelings to the headteachers. Under one-third felt well prepared; around three-quarters felt fairly well prepared and only one felt poorly prepared. This was not in the same school as the headteacher who felt poorly prepared.

By 1990 half of classteachers were feeling well prepared with the rest fairly well prepared. Nearly one-third were feeling much better prepared than the year before and two-thirds felt better prepared. Reasons given for this were predictably to do with familiarity and having had personal experience or having learnt from the personal experience of a colleague. There had also been a building up of resources and opportunities within courses and school based activities for planning.

By 1991, as with the headteachers, there was an apparent drop in confidence. Now just over one-third rather than one-half of class teachers reported feeling well prepared. Why should this have been? Between 1989 and 1990 the subjects that had been introduced were mathematics, science and English. Between 1990 and 1991 technology and Welsh were introduced. It may have been that these subjects were 'newer' in many respects than the earlier ones and this had led to the drop in confidence. The original orders in mathematics, science and English were already under review. Teachers may have felt that their efforts towards competency in those subjects were wasted. It may have been that teachers could see that soon more subjects (history and geography) would be added and that they would need to tackle an ever-broadening curriculum. It could have been that the adverse comments of politicians and the media left teachers feeling inadequately prepared for their teaching role in general. Whatever the cause, the drop in the level of confidence about preparation for teaching the National Curriculum was worrying.

Perceived Additional Needs

Headteachers and class teachers were also asked what support and resources they needed to implement the orders.

1989: Headteachers

In 1989 headteachers saw human resources as being most important. Equipment was the next priority with emphasis given to science equipment. Although calculators and computers were specifically mentioned in the mathematics orders only two headteachers mentioned them specifically. While this is not too surprising given the prominence given to computers within the LEA, there had been no marked adoption of calculators. The LEA had not been part of the Primary Initiatives in Mathematics Project (PRIME)[2] and there appeared to be marginal use of calculators in many schools. While six schools had computers available in every classroom and eight schools reported that they were in regular use, only two schools were using calculators regularly in mathematics lessons.

Support from LEA advisory staff was also seen as desirable by eight headteachers. Rather surprisingly in retrospect, the need for more time to carry out the tasks required by the National Curriculum was only mentioned by two headteachers.

1989: Class teachers

The class teachers placed strong emphasis on both human resources and equipment. In particular the extra human resources were seen in terms of supporting the assessment process.

> Can teachers teach and assess simultaneously?

> ... teaching support especially for assessment with split age classes.

In fact assessment and record keeping featured strongly.

> More time for assessment and record keeping.

> More support and training for assessment and record keeping in all areas.

> Tape recorders for taping children for assessment.

Technology, science and Welsh received specific mention alongside support for the teaching of the core subjects in terms of INSET, advisory teacher support and specialized equipment.

1990: Headteachers

In 1990 the emphasis had shifted away from human resources towards equipment. Once again science equipment was in most demand with technology now overtaking mathematics as the second need. INSET in Welsh, technology and assessment were mentioned as was continued support from the LEA advisory staff in terms of school based and centrally based INSET. There was still little interest in extra calculators or computers. However eleven schools reported change in their use of calculators compared with five reporting a change in their use of computers.

1990: Class teachers

In 1990 sixteen teachers specifically mentioned the need for 'an extra pair of hands' in the classroom. This was not specifically for the assessment procedures. Several teachers mentioned working with small groups. It appears that differentiation was now taking place and that teachers felt that children needed more individual teaching in order to 'achieve the ATs' (attainment targets).

Equipment for technology and computers received specific mention but once again it was the need for equipment for science (in particular expendable resources) that predominated.

Advisory support was seen as desirable but in terms of advice and discussion rather than criticism or written documentation.

Once again the need for specific support with the teaching of Welsh received mention.

1991: Headteachers

By 1991 the human resource emphasis had returned. The need was seen in terms of the classroom (pupil/teacher ratio, adult help, non-contact time) and in support from the LEA.

> [We need] more help from the advisers; [they are] rarely seen in schools today.

The Impact of the National Curriculum

> This school seriously needs additional support at infant level in basic subjects.

> [We need] advisory school based support for foundation [non-core] studies.

> Support [is] needed from advisors [and] advisory teachers to come to school to give encouragement to staff and help when needed.

Now that the assessments were being carried out a need was seen for extra staffing and time to allow for this.

> Teacher support for Y2 teacher [is needed] so that they can conduct the teacher assessment more fairly on a one to one basis and when involved in small group tasks.

> [An] additional teacher [is] required during SATs.

> Non-contact time to teach and assess individuals and small groups of children.

However there was still a need for other resources. What was noticeable was a new emphasis on money.

> A strong injection of cash would be appreciated!

> More money! We cannot buy new materials to implement all the new work developing from the National Curriculum.

> This year we have had to provide money from school funds to get books from the prescribed booklist for reading.

There were also pleas for time.

> [We need] time to consider where we are, what needs to be done and where we are going. After school is not the answer.

Preparing for the National Curriculum

[I need time] to digest all the new documents to enable me [headteacher] to support staff.

1991: Classteachers

Once again there was a strong need for human support within the classroom. Sometimes this was of the 'extra pair of hands' variety, sometimes it was in terms of smaller classes. This need was both to help with the teaching as well as to allow the assessment procedures to be undertaken. Welsh once again received specific mention for advisory teacher support and courses. The teachers too mentioned money in a way that they had not done before. Science equipment was again mentioned. Teachers also saw a need for books for teachers as well as pupils, particularly for non-core subjects.

One class teacher said that there was never enough money for the resources that were required in every subject. Another said that her school was well equipped both in human and material resources. It is not clear whether this was a difference in expectations or that the schools were in fact differently resourced.

Conclusions

The report by HMI (England) on in-service training for the introduction of the National Curriculum 1988–90 comments

> By the end of the report period the majority of teachers were better informed and more confident about implementing the core subjects of the National Curriculum. However, anxieties about assessment, recording and reporting were largely undiminished. The teachers' training needs changed once they had started to implement the National Curriculum by becoming more specifically related to the difficulties they were encountering. (DES, 1991: 9)

Barber and Graham (1993) attribute the substantial degree of success with which the National Curriculum has been implemented in part to LEAs.

> One [reason] is that LEAs, on the whole, have provided effective assistance, support and training to schools, yet their continued existence remains doubtful. All the evaluations of National Curriculum implementation are strongly positive about the role of the LEAs, and particularly their advisory or curriculum support teachers, have played.
> (Barber and Graham, 1993: 14)

This reflects the overall findings of the research project.

The initial feelings that teachers had of being overwhelmed with information were somewhat alleviated as it became apparent that the subject orders were not going to arrive simultaneously. We believe that it was the subsequent revision of the core subjects of mathematics and science that led to a drop in confidence.

Initially the requests for more resources were often tied in with concerns over the management of the assessment procedures. As these became more familiar the required resources were to do with aspects of the curriculum such as calculators for mathematics. Class teachers still looked for extra pairs of hands to help with wider aspects of teaching than formal assessment procedures. As might have been expected the particular subjects highlighted by teachers changed as new subject orders came on line. Emphasis on money increased as schools became more familiar with the implications of local financial management.

Teachers articulated concerns about assessment and record keeping in our research. This was also reported by Bennett *et al.* (1992) and Broadfoot *et al.* (1991a). These findings raise a number of questions regarding assessment including the following:

- Were their concerns partly fuelled by the emphasis that the LEA placed on assessment by focusing on INSET for this or was the LEA responding to the teachers' needs?
- What role did the emphasis in the media and by the politicians of the need for accountability and the role of the National Curriculum in raising standards play?
- How new was the notion of a formal assessment procedure to primary school teachers and, in particular, teachers of the rising 5-year-olds?

- Where did the emphasis lie between teacher assessment and the more formal SATs?

The fact that the LEA did focus much of the early INSET on the assessment side of the National Curriculum may in part account for the fact that the teachers reported feeling to some extent prepared in that area.

The next chapter which examines the teaching of the core subjects reports a strong feeling that it was in assessment and record keeping that most change took place.

Notes

1 SMILE was a mathematics curriculum development project set up in 1972 by the Inner London Education Authority.
2 The Primary Initiatives in Mathematics Education was a Schools Curriculum Development Committee (during the course of the project the work of this committee was taken over by the National Curriculum Council) funded project that ran from 1985 to 1989 and was based at Homerton College, Cambridge. It was directed by the late Hilary Shuard.

Chapter 4

Teaching The National Curriculum

Introduction

This chapter reports some effects of the structure and content of the National Curriculum on the teaching at Key Stage 1. Although traditionally there has been some discrete subject teaching in the primary school even at Key Stage 1 (mathematics, music and PE for example) there has been a strong emphasis on the teaching of themes and topics without subject boundaries. Within the LEA in which we did our research the advisory service held a strong commitment to such an approach. Although not all teachers embraced the approach with equal enthusiasm, often because the message was picked up as the dogmatic interpretation that everything should be taught through the thematic approach, there was an overall sympathy with cross-curricular teaching. A concern voiced early on in the life of the National Curriculum was the effect that single-subject orders might have on such approaches. It was obvious to us that this should be a focus of our research.

The choice of science as a core subject alongside English (or Welsh) and mathematics, while not particularly controversial, was a change in emphasis. This then led us to another important area for research.

Class Teachers and the Core Subjects[1]

This section considers the class teachers' views first because they were actively involved with the day to day teaching. Headteachers' views are considered later as their responses may be seen to be also concerned with policy and informed by a variety of elements as well as personal experience. There are also more comments from class teachers than headteachers. This reflects the results of the interviews.

In 1989 the teachers were asked questions about the planning, organization, assessment and record keeping of various subjects. They were then asked to predict the effects of the National Curriculum in mathematics, English, Welsh and science. We were interested in particular in how they thought their day to day class-based work would be affected. We asked them specific questions about thematic and cross-curricular work. In 1990 the class teachers were in general asked the same questions again but this time they were asked to reflect on the effects that the National Curriculum had had on their work. A comparison of their projections and reflections follows.

In 1989 class teachers felt that the greatest impact of the National Curriculum would come in the areas of record keeping and assessment. This was fairly consistent across the subjects with mathematics and science being seen as likely to be marginally more affected than English and Welsh. In science and Welsh the message was that teachers were expecting major change. However in English and mathematics there was little difference between the numbers of teachers expecting minor change and those expecting a more substantial change. If we think about the traditional role of English and mathematics in our English-medium primary schools this is understandable. The time and energy put into record keeping focused on the 'Basics', the three Rs, in other words English and mathematics. The approach to science and Welsh was less formal, less firmly structured and hence there was less emphasis on assessment and record keeping.

> Assessment and record keeping of science has been very informal and sketchy in the past.

> We have no real science assessment at the present.

> Records [in science] will need to be more detailed and individual.

> Very little [science] is recorded at present.

The Impact of the National Curriculum

> The main change will be in assessment and record keeping since it is so difficult to assess science with infants — so much depends on the teacher's knowledge of individual children — I fear that these professional skills may be lost if everything has to be formally recorded.

With Welsh the trend seemed to be very informal with four teachers stating that no written records were kept at present. Five teachers reported that there was no Welsh for infants at all.

Time allocation to Welsh is very haphazard at present.

There will be lots of change overall since the approach has always been rather vague.

Reflecting in 1990 the teachers felt that the impact had been less than they had envisaged in all subjects but particularly so in science and Welsh. Eighteen teachers reported that record keeping and assessment in Welsh still needed to be developed as no formal records were kept. This obviously had not been prioritized as a task and therefore the teachers had not noticed a change. It appears that the main energies were put into the development of science teaching with seventeen teachers reporting more (time being spent on?) science teaching than before and hence there was less impact on the other subjects than teachers had envisaged.

However in mathematics nine teachers reported that assessment and record keeping had changed and was now more detailed. One teacher speculated

> I wonder what more this detail really tells you about a child's progress?

Two teachers reported that they had always kept detailed records of mathematics and these had been easy to adapt for the National Curriculum.

In English the emphasis appeared to be on an increase in record keeping.

The changes in record keeping varied from subject to

subject. In English and mathematics where records may have been kept in the past they were now more detailed and directly related to the National Curriculum attainment targets. In science and Welsh, where it was much less likely that records had been kept, formal detailed records were developed.

Assessment became more formalized and detailed with teachers anticipating the style of the standardized assessment tasks that would be introduced in 1989/90. Teachers were quite used to assessing pupils' performance in some areas of English and mathematics. The same was not true for science or second language Welsh. The teachers would have to transfer skills developed in assessing reading, arithmetic etc., to the assessment of communication, using and applying mathematics, etc. as well as to science and Welsh.

In 1989 teachers had envisaged that their classroom organization and teaching methods would only change in a minor way or not at all and this was what they felt had happened when asked to reflect in 1990. When reporting what type of changes had taken place, teachers tended to comment on the allocation of time to different subjects and to some slight adjustment of methods to include more practical work.

> I am now doing more practical work in science hence there has been some change in organization, time spent and teaching methods.

> In order to fit in the science some of the maths [*sic*] time has been reduced.

> ... more time spent on practical activities [in mathematics] hence a change in teaching methods and organization — it takes more time to organize and carry out.

> To be meaningful science needs to be done in small groups; this takes more time.

> Plenty of practical work has always been school policy.

> There's been no real change in time or methods.

The Impact of the National Curriculum

When it came to considering the curriculum in terms of content and time allocation the teachers had envisaged minor or no changes in English and mathematics with more change in science and major changes in Welsh.

> We will need more time for core subjects to cover the work.

> We will need more time for observing throughout the year.

> I'm recording everything at present due to the fact that I'm unsure what is expected. Eventually I will know what to record/what not to record.

In 1990 more teachers felt there had been changes in English and mathematics and even more in science. In Welsh fewer had perceived a change than had been expecting it. Once again this suggests to us that the energies had focused on science.

In 1989 there was a tendency for teachers to think that they would not have to change their teaching methods — although they were split equally between no change and some change in the teaching of English. A third were expecting change in mathematics.

> More investigative work will have to take place than at present — this is bound to affect the teaching of mathematics.

> More practical work, more problem solving [AT1 and 8].

A third were expecting major changes in the teaching of science and Welsh. Up to then Welsh appears to have been taught informally or by visiting teachers.

In 1990 very few teachers reported major changes in their teaching methods. This contrasts with the findings of the Primary Assessment Curriculum and Experience (PACE) team. In 1990 45 per cent of their teachers perceived some loss of autonomy over teaching methods. However nearly half felt no change in their freedom to select teaching methods. (Osborn *et al.* 1993)

In Welsh nearly two-thirds reported no change at all. The changes that were reported were in the area of planning.

> The only changes will be to include all attainment targets when planning — a great deal of Welsh is done cross-curricularly already.

In science over a third of the teachers reported some change but over another third reported no change. The reported changes were an increase in practical work and more detailed planning.

> Every child does practical work for every experiment. Previously the class teacher may have demonstrated and the children observed.

> The class teacher needs to be more aware and plan in more detail.

In mathematics nearly one-half felt that they had made no changes at all with an identical number reporting some change. Those changes too mentioned practical work.

> ... more practical work now — everything else has just been altered slightly to meet the National Curriculum requirements.

> I now do more games, discussions and investigational work.

> There's more discussion before and after the activity now.

In English nearly one-half reported some change with just over one-third reporting no change. The changes in English teaching were more varied than those reported above. The comments reported below give a flavour of that variety.

The Impact of the National Curriculum

> Nothing drastic!
>
> ... more time on drama and listening skills.
>
> ... not as structured as it was.
>
> With a split class [mixed age] I feel I'm pushing them further to meet the attainment targets.
>
> The school has decided to drop the reading scheme so all the work is now centred on the topic.
>
> ... much more language work based on picture books.

The class teachers were contacted again in 1991. They were asked to comment on any problems or difficulties they had experienced in the implementation of the National Curriculum in the same four subjects. Four out of five teachers reported no difficulties or problems in implementing English. A very large majority also reported no problems or difficulties with the implementation of the mathematics National Curriculum but two teachers mentioned that they felt that there was too much to cover in-depth in the time available. However over one-third reported some problems or difficulties with the implementation of the science curriculum.

Two teachers felt that some attainment targets, e.g. AT 10 Level 3 (*sic*) were not easily achievable.

> Some of the attainment targets were difficult for children to understand.

Four teachers reported a lack of equipment and five teachers felt there were too many attainment targets.

> There are too many attainment targets to cover them in any depth.
>
> There are too many attainment targets to ensure depth as well as breadth.

Some non-Welsh speaking class teachers (six) made comments about their own deficiencies such as:

I'm not very good but I'm learning.

As a non-Welsh speaker it is difficult to extend the children's vocabulary or their fluency or sentence construction.

I'm relying on the peripatetic teacher too much.

I'm English born and bred!

Despite this very nearly all teachers reported no problems or difficulties with implementing the Welsh curriculum.

It appears that three years into the National Curriculum teachers had found the implementation of English, mathematics and science less problematic than they had envisaged at first. This perhaps supports the NCC's 'teething problems' theory (NCC, 1993a: 7). Non-Welsh speakers felt that they were struggling somewhat with the Welsh but this is understanable given their lack of knowledge and skill.

The Headteachers' Views

The headteachers were asked in 1989 to predict the effects of the National Curriculum in each of the four core subjects. As with the class teachers the headteachers were expecting the biggest change to be in connection with Welsh but when they reflected in 1990 it was in science that they had perceived the greatest change. Overall it was with record keeping and assessment that they were consistently expecting the most changes and in 1990 it was with record keeping and assessment of science and Welsh that the headteachers felt there had been the greatest changes. There were also changes in record keeping in English and mathematics but there was more of a balance/spread as to the extent of the change. There was much less change reported in the curriculum, class organization and teaching methods in Welsh and

English. The responses in mathematics were more or less balanced between no change and some change. In science the emphasis was towards some change with much change in the curriculum being more commonly reported. Other than in science, headteachers observed less change in the curriculum than they had expected in 1989.

With English nearly two-thirds of the headteachers were expecting no change in classroom organization with all of them expecting change in assessment methods and record keeping. Nearly one-third were expecting no change in teaching methods and three-quarters expecting change in the curriculum. In 1990 half reported no change in curriculum, class organization or teaching methods and all of them reported change in assessment and record keeping.

In mathematics one-third were expecting no change in the curriculum, one-half no change in teaching methods, with all expecting change in assessment and all but one change in record keeping. In 1990 more reported no change in teaching methods; the other reports were more or less consistent with the predictions.

In science the greatest change between 1989 and 1990 was in classroom organization with two-thirds of headteachers predicting some change in 1989; whereas in 1990 one quarter actually reported that much change had taken place.

In Welsh there was much less change reported in curriculum, classroom organization and teaching methods than had been predicted. Nearly all headteachers reported change in record keeping and assessment although the emphasis shifted slightly from much change to some change.

The details of the changes the headteachers reported in all of the above were similar to those reported by the class teachers: more formalized or new assessment methods; more detail in the record keeping; and organizational changes driven by the need to find time for new subjects or new elements of existing subjects.

> There is now more variety and practical work; teaching methods have had to change to accommodate this.

> Assessment in English has to take account of all the attainment targets.

Science is now an integral part of infant work whereas previously it was much more incidental.

In the past science was much less structured.

There was no real assessment or record keeping in science before the National Curriculum.

Record keeping is now much more detailed [in mathematics].

There is more emphasis on problem solving and games [in mathematics] than before.

Welsh will be brought into as many aspects of cross-curricular work as possible.

Teaching methods [in Welsh] will remain mainly oral with some written work.

Thematic Work

As well as following reactions to the individual subjects teachers and headteachers were asked about cross-curricular/thematic/topic work. One aspect of topic work for consideration is what curriculum subjects are touched by the topic work. This is subtly different from 'teaching' a curriculum subject through a topic, thematic or cross-curricular approach. For example many topics include the use of mathematical skills such as the drawing of graphs. Sometimes a new type of graph, pie charts for example, will be introduced using data gathered from the topic. On other occasions the children will have learnt how to draw pie charts by using their published mathematics scheme with some data provided by the authors and later they will use that skill to display data collected as part of a topic. In its 1992 review of primary education CCW (1992c) reported that, in general, skill getting was achieved with discrete teaching and skill usage was practised in topic work (p. 17).

The Impact of the National Curriculum

Class Teachers' Views

Teachers were asked how often certain subjects were included in the planning of topic work. We did not ask them to distinguish between use or consolidation of skills and concepts and the introduction of new skills or concepts.

In 1989 thirty teachers responded. Twenty-nine always included English and mathematics, twenty-eight science, twenty-seven expressive arts, twenty environmental studies, nineteen religious education and nine (including two in Welsh-medium schools) Welsh in their topic planning. Five never included Welsh and one teaching in a Welsh-medium school never included English in their planning. The English-medium schools included Welsh to varying degrees: seven always, five frequently, six sometimes, five rarely and five never.

In 1990 thirty-three class teachers responded. There was little change in the inclusion of English, mathematics and science. However now twenty-two teachers were always including Welsh in their topic planning. One was including it frequently, six sometimes, five rarely and five never. Expressive arts had dropped to nineteen always including it, four frequently, two sometimes and one rarely. Environmental studies was included to more or less the same extent as in 1989. Religious education had changed slightly with twenty-two including it always, four frequently and seven sometimes.

In 1989 three-quarters of the teachers were expecting that the National Curriculum would affect their cross-curricular approach. However the majority of those were only expecting that there would be minor changes. Two-fifths of the schools stressed that they were already using a thematic approach. One-fifth were adamant that the National Curriculum would not affect that thematic approach.

> This school already runs a thematic approach to teaching and this will not change.

There, however, were feelings that the thematic work would have to become more focused.

Teaching the National Curriculum

> It should not affect it but teachers will have to be careful to relate what is being done to what is required by the National Curriculum.

> There will have to be more precise planning.

> We will need to think in subject areas in order to achieve targets; that is work out a flow chart around a theme but split it into subjects to ensure that all attainment targets are covered.

> It is going to be easier to link maths [sic] and language into a science topic linked to the National Curriculum therefore there might be less choice [of subjects] than before.

> Themes which cover attainment targets in core subjects will obviously be chosen in preference to others.

> In the past we have always been able to choose freely, now we will be selecting with attainment targets in mind.

In 1990 teachers' reflections were similar to their 1989 predictions. Well over three-quarters reported some effect on their cross-curricular approach with well over one-half of those teachers reporting little change. Under one-fifth reported no change at all. Practically half of the teachers commented on the need to relate this work to attainment targets. There was support for the view that work *had* to be cross-curricular in order to cover the National Curriculum.

> I am more aware of the need for a cross-curricular approach. How else would teachers fit everything in?

However one teacher reported:

> It is difficult to cover the whole range of activities within the thematic approach — some have to be taught separately.

The Impact of the National Curriculum

There was also a feeling that the choice of topic or theme *was* now constrained.

> Themes are laid down now whereas prior to the National Curriculum the class teacher could chose her [sic] own theme — now if she wants to change them she has to consult the other infant staff.

> Now I chose a theme on science and fit the other curriculum areas to it. I felt free before. Now I'm constrained in my choice.

The Headteachers' Views

There was only marginal change in headteachers' views about a thematic approach between 1989 and 1990 with the vast majority predicting and then recording little or some change, with a small number recording no change or substantial change.

In 1990 headteachers were also asked if they expected a shift in the balance between cross-curricular and subject specialist work. Over one-half replied no and over one-third replied yes.

In 1992 CCW (1992c) reported:

> While many schools approached the issue [planning] thematically, some because it was the method currently favoured by HMI Inspectorate [sic] and the advisory service, others explained that a broad theme moving towards a more subject specific delivery was being used more frequently . . . in many cases schools were committed to the ideology of working thematically. (p. 16)

In 1993 OFSTED (1993a) went further: 'The vast majority of primary schools remain firmly committed to grouping different subjects together to be taught as topics' (para. 7).

Back in 1990 the headteachers reported:

> Staff feel the pull towards subject based teaching.

> Where NC requirements don't fit in naturally with themes these must be covered separately.

Teaching the National Curriculum

It is not possible to teach via a subject approach. Teachers would be swamped and not able to keep track of what children were getting out of it. With a thematic approach teachers will know what's been touched upon.

Most work will be covered within topics but there may be occasions when subjects will have to be taught as one-offs.

It's difficult to answer until we know what history and geography require.

When headteachers were questioned in 1991 about the shift from cross-curricular work 50 per cent were now reporting a shift.

Attainment targets not covered in the theme are taught separately. The introduction of the National Curriculum subjects makes the integration of these into one theme extremely difficult if not impossible. We are concerned that the view that subject basics cannot be tackled in a thematic approach is spreading. We are trying for a balance between what is integrated and what must be done separately.

The NC itself being subject orientated has not helped — we continue a thematic approach but with core subject areas being dealt with in a more subject orientated fashion.

The balance has been to science over the last three years. This might well change to history and geography this coming year.

In 1992 CCW (1992c) reported that the most common approaches to planning were:

- subject specific topics developed within themes, e.g. history in particular, also geography;

- subject specific topics used to fill in gaps, to reinforce, used as mini topics;
- discrete subject planning as more subjects come on-stream, e.g. maths, science and some English;
- linking the broad theme to individual schemes of work (the topic web!). (para. 7)

Conclusions

The introduction of the National Curriculum appears to have affected the teaching of core subjects mainly in the areas of assessment and record keeping. Some teachers also reported changes in their methods of teaching and classroom organization to accommodate the subject order requirements, for example, more practical work in mathematics and science. Despite past rhetoric of CCW and advisers, headteachers were noticing a shift away from cross-curricular work as did OFSTED (1993a: 6):

> Over the year however there was a noticeable shift towards designing topics that were more focused on a single subject such as history or science; fewer schools than previously used broad topics to teach all or most of the subjects.

Classteachers were reporting (as did CCW in 1992c: 17) much more structuring of topic work to take in as much National Curriculum work as possible.

There was also evidence of a trend towards science led topics although CCW reports (1992c: 16) (after the introduction of the history and geography orders) that the trend is towards topics led by those subjects. CCW (1992c) reported that

> In more than a few primary schools there were differences in the approaches used at infant and junior level. Subject specific tasks were used less frequently in infant schools who were more likely to plan over the whole of KS1.

It is possible that our primary school headteachers were reporting more generally about the 4–11 phase than specifically about Key Stage 1.

There is a consensus then between our research, CCW's consultation findings and those reported by OFSTED. There is already a move away from thematic/cross-curricular work towards discrete subject teaching, topics are no longer broad multi-subject studies but tend to focus on science or history or geography.

The key questions arising from our research and reports both formal and informal are

1. Are there similar trends in the impact on the teaching of core subjects and the thematic approach in Key Stage 1 and Key Stage 2?
2. Are these trends continuing, becoming more pronounced or returning to the pre-National Curriculum status quo?
3. How are single subject/specialist teaching and cross-curricular work viewed now?

We address these questions in Chapter 9.

Note

1. We have included Welsh alongside English, mathematics and science because of its dual role as both a core and non-core subject. When comments refer to Welsh-medium schools this will be made explicit.

Chapter 5

Differentiating the National Curriculum

In this chapter we examine ways in which teachers in the sample sought to differentiate their teaching so as to meet the perceived needs of their individual pupils with regard to their differing age, maturity or ability levels. Further we look at the impact of the National Curriculum on this process of differentiation as judged by the teachers. The findings are presented under the following headings:

> Differentiation in free play activities;
> Teaching under-5s;
> Differentiation according to ability:
> > The class teachers' views on the teaching of more able learners and slower learners;
> > The headteachers' views on the teaching of more able learners and slower learners.

Differentiation in Free Play Activities

During their interviews prior to the introduction of the National Curriculum the Year 1 class teachers were asked the following questions concerning free play in their classrooms:

1. On average during each day how much time does each child spend in free play activities?
2. Does this vary according to the age or ability of each child?
3. Does this amount change over the course of each year?
4. What role do you take in these free play activities?

Differentiating the National Curriculum

5   Are these activities linked to the more formal work in the various curriculum areas?

These questions were repeated approximately one year later during the first year of the implementation of the new curriculum.

In the following presentation of findings it should be remembered that, while the majority of the teachers were responsible for either a single age class (5 to 6-year-olds) or a twin age group (4 to 6-year-olds), a minority of teachers taught classes with a wider age range, from 4 to 7-year-olds.

On average, in both years, the children spent between one half hour to one hour daily in free play activities, although some teachers were unable to quantify the amount which fluctuated for various reasons. In both years most of the teachers stated that the amount of time spent in free play varied according to the age and ability of each child. Where there was a mixed age range in the class the younger children, particularly the under-5s, would spend more time in free play and several teachers reported that, as children developed during the year and were increasingly able to tackle more structured work they spent less time in free play. As one teacher put it:

The older they get the less they play and the more formal their work becomes their need for play is less.

However there seemed to be some divergence of practice regarding the amount of free play time accorded to the slower developing, 'less able' children. In those classrooms where the opportunities for free play were conditional upon the children completing teacher directed tasks beforehand, the slower children were reported as spending less time in free play than their age peers. In contrast some other teachers made a point of giving these children *additional* free play since their ability to carry out more formal work was limited. In the words of one of these teachers:

The poorer ability children play more, the brighter pupils move towards work which demands more of them.

Despite this concern to meet the perceived developmental needs of the slower learning children the introduction of the National Curriculum appeared to reduce the teacher's scope to allow them more free play time, at least in some classrooms. The following comments express some teachers' concern at this trend:

> Children now have a lot less free play than before the National Curriculum as the result of the teacher cramming in work.
>
> Play time has decreased due to National Curriculum demands and this can be detrimental to some pupils who need to play to learn social skills and to develop language.
>
> Slow pupils [now] work most of the time in order to meet attainment targets. Before the National Curriculum they played much more in order to develop language and oral skills.
>
> Less able children spend more time on work but really they are the ones who need more play.

In some other classrooms though, despite the need to work towards the National Curriculum attainment targets, the teachers were able to continue to arrange for slower learning children to have more opportunities for free play than their peers. One teacher, for example, said that she required them to complete fewer teacher directed tasks than the more able children before being allowed to engage in free play. This was done in order to motivate them to complete the more structured tasks.

In both years nearly all of the teachers reported that their children's free play activities were linked to the more formal curriculum at least sometimes. This linking took various forms and ranged across the whole curriculum. For example, children might act out a scene from a novel they had been studying in their English curriculum. Similarly their sand and water play and their constructional play with Unifix, Multilink or Lego bricks was thought to help them in developing important mathematical concepts.

Differentiating the National Curriculum

One-third of the teachers mentioned that the children's free play sometimes reflected a topic being dealt with in their more formal work, as when setting up a classroom shop following a visit to a supermarket. However there was some disagreement among the teachers regarding the principle of deliberately linking free play with the more formal curriculum. Those rejecting the principle made comments such as:

Free play is linked to topic work occasionally but in the main free play is exactly that.

Play is not part of the forward planning of the class teacher.

The teachers appeared to vary widely in the extent to which they became directly involved in their children's free play activities. A number of them used free play times as an opportunity to listen to children reading or for teaching groups of children. A few expressed the view that free play should be kept as free as possible from 'adult interference', other than to sort out disputes or to encourage children to engage in some form of free play activity if they were not doing so. Other teachers seemed to be more actively involved in the free play activities insofar as their time allowed this. Such involvement ranged from directly observing the children's free play to advising and helping them in their play and initiating such activities where necessary. When observed, good social behaviour would be praised and encouraged. Teachers might engage in discussions with children in the free play context in order to develop their language.

Clearly those teachers fortunate enough to have the regular help of a nursery assistant or other qualified aide were in a much better position to support their children's free play activities if their wished to do so, although this point did not actually arise in our interviews with them.

There was relatively little explicit reference by the teachers to the impact of the National Curriculum on the nature of their professional involvement in their children's free play. One commented that she now sometimes deliberately structured a free play activity so as to work toward a particular attainment target and two other teachers reported that they now had much less time to sit with children as they played, due to the demands of the National Curriculum upon them.

In summary, during the year following the introduction of the National Curriculum, there did not appear to be a major shift in the amount of time devoted to free play, the extent to which it was linked to more formal teaching, or in the nature of the teacher's involvement in it. Nevertheless the class teachers reported a decrease in the amount of time available for free play and some of them were particularly concerned about the adverse consequences of this for the development of slower learning children.

Teaching Under-5s

The Views of the Class Teachers

Approximately one year after the introduction of the National Curriculum the class teachers were asked at interview what effect they felt the National Curriculum had had on the teaching of children under age 5. Such children would have been in separate reception classes for 4 to 5-year-olds in the medium sized or large infant schools/departments, but in the smaller schools, they would be taught alongside 5-year-olds (Year 1) and sometimes older children (see Chapter 2). Of the thirty-four teachers involved at this time, twenty-seven did not have any under-fives in their classes and therefore did not respond to the question.

The comments of the seven remaining teachers referred to both positive and negative effects of the National Curriculum upon the teaching of these children, although a few teachers stated that there had been no noticeable effect since the children worked at their own level. Regarding benefits, one teacher felt that starting the National Curriculum at a younger age would benefit the child in the long run. Another teacher said that, while she felt that she expected too much of this group because they were in a class with older pupils, it could be an advantage for them since they were developing alongside the Year 1 pupils and they progressed toward the attainment targets despite their age. The latter teacher clearly felt that the younger children could be subjected

Differentiating the National Curriculum

to some pressure towards the achievement of attainment targets as did a number of other teachers.

Further feedback from class teachers on the question of the effect of the National Curriculum upon under-5s came from a seminar held by the authors in the summer of 1993. The twenty-four infant teachers who attended came from several LEAs within the region and one or two of them came from schools that had participated in the study. The teachers were put into small groups to discuss several questions, including the effect of the National Curriculum upon under-5s. In contrast to the somewhat mixed responses to this question from the teachers in our study reported above, the teachers in the seminar groups reported predominantly adverse consequences for under-5s. These included the premature formalization of the curriculum for these children and increased pressure upon them to work towards the achievement of National Curriculum attainment targets. Such pressure had led to a reduction in their opportunities for free play and less time for their teachers to talk with them and thereby help to enrich their language.

Particularly worrying was the increased emphasis reported by these teachers upon the production of written work by the children. As one group commented

> The National Curriculum has influenced our perception of what is respectable, bona fide work.

Another group described the 'worksheet syndrome' which was now squeezing out forms of learning, including the more practical, which the teachers regarded as being of higher quality. Such formalization of their learning could cause children to come to dislike school, it was thought.

Finally there was some reference to the negative effects on this age group of the heavy preoccupation of some infant teachers with the administration of SATs during the summer term. According to one group this created tensions within the (mixed age) classroom and a possibly adverse environment for the younger children. Whereas the summer term was traditionally a period of rapid development for infants, including under-5s, it was now largely occupied with SATs in mixed age classes.

The Impact of the National Curriculum

The Views of the Headteachers

In their interviews the headteachers were not asked any questions directly about children's free play activities but, in the second interview, and in the written follow-up questionnaire they completed one year later, they were asked about the effect of the National Curriculum upon the teaching of the under-5-year-olds in their schools, whether in Year 1 or in nursery or reception classes. In 1990 approximately one-third of them felt that little or no change had occurred in such teaching following the introduction of the National Curriculum. By 1991, this proportion had risen to over half of the group. Comments from this group were along the following lines:

> Individual children are given work to do regardless of age. The National Curriculum has not changed this;

> With mixed age classes the children have always followed the same curriculum as older children but at their own level and this has not changed with the introduction of the National Curriculum;

> The quality remains intact and is being developed. The classroom atmosphere remains warm and friendly with all committed to the various tasks.

Some of these headteachers spoke of the pre-5 curriculum (including nursery education) as preparing children for Key Stage 1. One headteacher went further than this by announcing that the school would be making a start with the Key Stage 1 curriculum for the under-5s in the reception class later that year. Another commented as follows concerning this age group:

> They have started work on the National Curriculum and a far more structured approach has resulted.

The responses of the remaining headteachers to this question mentioned both the benefits and the possible dangers to the under-5s of the introduction of the National Curriculum. The benefits

Differentiating the National Curriculum

noted included a broader curriculum, with more science than previously and more confident teaching associated with this. The dangers concerned the premature introduction of very young children to more formal, National Curriculum-led teaching. One headteacher, for example, expressed the fear of starting the National Curriculum too early.

> The aims and needs of the individual child in early childhood education should be protected. They should be allowed to progress at their own rate of development.

Another felt that care should be taken not to 'turn off' 4-year-olds by an over-emphasis upon written work. The teaching headteacher of a class of 3 to 7-year-olds, worried by the problem of catering for the under-5-year-olds in such a situation had decided to split the class in the afternoons, with the latter forming a separate teaching group. Such views regarding the need to preserve the distinctive, 'child centred' character of the teaching of pre-5 children appear to contrast with the view of other headteachers, illustrated earlier, that a firmer structuring of the curriculum, following the introduction of the National Curriculum, was to be welcomed for these children.

One or two headteachers expressed concern about the effects of formalizing the curriculum for pre-5 children from disadvantaged home backgrounds. The following comment echoes the worry of some class teachers, reported earlier, that the introduction of the National Curriculum had resulted in less free play for these children:

> Too much is demanded of our young pupils who do not receive a lot of parental support. A lot of time was spent previously on social skills, constructive play and developing relationships. However, as a result of the National Curriculum there is insufficient time for this nowadays and pupils have to develop these skills and attitudes at the same time as they are being pressured to progress through levels of attainment.

In summary, while only one-third to one-half of the headteachers reported any impact of the National Curriculum upon the teaching of children under 5, opinion was sharply divided amongst them as to whether this was positive or negative. Those stressing its benefits described the firmer structuring of the curriculum that had resulted, while others viewed the National Curriculum as a threat to the distinctive, child centred nature of the early years' curriculum. The latter view was reinforced by the conclusions of a group of infant teachers attending an INSET seminar after the completion of the study. These teachers reported that their under-5 pupils were being subjected to more formal work in preparation for the National Curriculum, with a consequent reduction in their opportunities for free play, talk, and various practical activities.

Differentiation According to Ability

As reported in Chapter 2 the majority of Year 1 classes represented in the study sample contained either 5 to 6-year-old children only or the latter group plus 'reception infants' aged 4 to 5-years old. Despite this concentration in age the range of children's academic attainment appeared to be wide.

During their interviews prior to and following the introduction of the National Curriculum the Year 1 class teachers were asked about the extent to which they individualized the curriculum and their teaching methods to meet the individual learning needs of their children. Many teachers claimed to be doing this 'always' or 'as much as possible', whether in the context of whole class or group teaching. Such individualization of work was clearly essential for those teachers in small schools whose infant classes catered for a very wide age range. It took the form of either allowing children to work at their own pace and level on tasks set for the whole class or of the setting of different tasks by the teacher according to the children's abilities or attainments. The latter was achieved partly through the use of published schemes for the core subjects and also, for some teachers, by the preparation of work cards or work sheets specially designed for individual children or groups.

In their interviews before the introduction of the National Curriculum both the Year 1 class teachers and the headteachers

Differentiating the National Curriculum

were asked what effect the National Curriculum might have on the more able children and the slower learning children in their classes, including those with special educational needs respectively. At interview in the following year they were asked to judge the effect of the introduction of the National Curriculum upon these groups of children in the light of their experience of teaching it for a year. In addition the headteachers, but not the class teachers, were asked to report the effects of teaching the National Curriculum on these children after a further year, in a written follow-up questionnaire. The views of the class teachers and of the headteachers will be reported separately and then compared.

The Class Teachers' Views

More able learners
Half of the class teachers expected the introduction of the National Curriculum to have little or no effect upon their teaching of the more able children, claiming that all infants work at their own individual rates and that the more able children were already fully extended. The other half anticipated that there would be some effect or made no prediction, perhaps reserving their judgment. Some of the latter teachers thought that the National Curriculum attainment targets would provide examples of how to stretch the more able children, making it easier to plan for their needs. Their comments included the following:

> They will succeed by following a curriculum which will stretch and enrich them.

> They will be pushed further because the National Curriculum will give the teacher direction.

Another prediction was that the wider content and variety of work in the new curriculum would create interest amongst these children.

One year later approximately half of the teachers judged that the introduction of the National Curriculum had had little or no effect upon the more able children in their classes; a similar proportion to those predicting such an outcome, as reported above. Again, there were comments from some teachers to the effect that these children would always cope whatever was presented to them. Those reporting observable effects mainly mentioned positive benefits, in particular the richer variety of subject matter to which the children were exposed, including more science and the greater opportunity for pupils to carry out investigations themselves. Teacher benefits included the tighter curriculum planning which gave them more direction in extending the more able children and the improved quality of teacher teamwork and staff collaborative planning.

There were relatively few negative effects noted and these centred on the pressure placed on the children and their teachers to cover the new extended curriculum and the possible danger that the more able pupils might suffer a loss of teacher attention as teachers spent more time with slower learning pupils in order to help them achieve their attainment targets. On the whole, therefore, the teachers' original predictions of either no significant impact, or mainly beneficial effects of the introduction of the National Curriculum on the teaching of more able pupils appeared to be borne out, at least in their own judgment.

Slower learners
It was pointed out in Chapter 2 that over half of the class teachers in the study judged that they had some children in their classes whom they suspected of having special educational needs, although very few children had been formally statemented.

With regard to slower learning children, including those with recognized special educational needs, approximately half of the teachers did not expect that the introduction of the National Curriculum would significantly affect them since they were judged to be fully catered for within the existing curriculum.

The consequences predicted by some of the remaining teachers were almost entirely negative, reflecting their concern about these children's capacities to cope with the increased demands of the new curriculum, as illustrated in the following comments:

Differentiating the National Curriculum

> I wonder if they will get lost in the work load. How do you get children who cannot read and write to do the work required?

> When Welsh becomes compulsory [in Wales] it could cause problems. They find it difficult enough to cope with number and English.

Other concerns focused upon the possibly damaging effects on these children's self-esteem of being labelled as failures at an early age with regard to the meeting of attainment targets, and upon the increased demands likely to be made on the teacher in helping the slower learners to achieve them.

One year later only three teachers reported that the introduction of the National Curriculum had had little effect upon the slower learning children, in contrast to the larger number (approximately half) of teachers who had predicted this, as reported above. For the remaining majority of teachers the observed impact of the National Curriculum was broadly in line with the earlier predictions of mainly negative consequences. There were frequent references to the greater curriculum pressure on these children to achieve the National Curriculum attainment targets with the result that the teachers were having to push them harder than before at the expense of the quality of the children's conceptual grasp and the degree of their skill mastery. The following comments illustrate these negative effects:

> I worry about pushing the slow learners too hard without going through the stages of learning a concept just to meet the attainment target.

> They receive a wider range of subject matter but may be put under more pressure than they should be to meet the attainment targets and are possibly not given enough time to absorb ideas fully before moving on to the next stage.

A small number of teachers reported that some of their slower learning children could not always comply with the demands of the new curriculum and were struggling to meet the new pressures upon them, for example, by not finishing set tasks and consequently having less time for free play. One teacher found herself unable to spend as much time with these children as before and worried a great deal about this. As in the interviews held one year previously some teachers expressed concern about the damaging effect on a child of a formal signalling of the failure to reach a particular attainment target.

> There is no safety net built in. The slower child will be labelled earlier on.

Despite the predominantly negative nature of the perceived consequences for slower learners of the introduction of the National Curriculum, there were some observations of benefits. One teacher commented that they were stretched more than before and experienced a richer curriculum at their level which included science and technology. Another felt that the National Curriculum made it easier for the teacher to see the next logical step in the teaching sequence, while the explicit sequence of attainment targets and their levels was seen as a benefit by the teacher who made the following remark:

> The National Curriculum makes the class teacher more aware of what slower learning children cannot do when it is all set out in front of you.

The importance of parental support for children's learning was expressed in the following comment by one of the teachers:

> It depends very much on the home background and parental support. The National Curriculum has had no real effect on their performance or the work presented to them. Children who receive support at home tend to make more progress than those who don't.

Finally one teacher appeared to adopt a somewhat philosophical attitude to the pressure to get these children to reach the relevant attainment targets.

Differentiating the National Curriculum

It may be better to spend more time discussing and talking with these children and training them to concentrate rather than worrying about covering attainment targets.

The Headteachers' Views

More able learners
When asked to predict the impact of the National Curriculum upon the more able children in the interview; prior to its introduction; well under half of the headteachers (nine) expected it to have little or no effect, citing similar reasons to those given by the class teachers to the same question reported earlier; for example, that the school was already catering fully for children's individual needs or that more able children will cope with anything whatever method or curriculum is employed. A similar number of headteachers expected the National Curriculum to bring some benefits to these children for a variety of reasons. These included: the possibility of accelerating the pace of their learning through the National Curriculum, perhaps with the help of secondary school teachers; a sharper focus upon individual capability than before which would enable children to reach their full potential and attain higher levels of attainment; and the motivational benefits of carrying out more investigative, problem solving work. Benefits to the class teachers were expected to come from the curriculum planning guidance provided by the National Curriculum, particularly with regard to planning for progression.

Only four headteachers thought there might be possible adverse effects. These included the danger that the more able children would not be so fully extended as before since the teacher might now pitch her or his teaching more at the average ability level of the class, threatening the concept of mixed ability teaching. Other comments referred to the prescriptive nature of the new curriculum which might reduce the opportunities for more able children to follow their own interests.

After one year of implementing the National Curriculum approximately half of the headteachers (fourteen) judged that it had made little or no impact upon the learning of the more able pupils. Their comments echoed those reported above in support of this predicted outcome, stressing the adaptability of these children in their learning. A few headteachers wished to reserve judgment after only one year and the number reporting positive outcomes was lower than expected on the basis of the earlier predictions. One of the latter headteachers commented that all children had benefited through working at their own levels in each curriculum area, while others mentioned the curricular planning benefits predicted earlier. As one headteacher put it,

> By the teacher examining each [curriculum] area in turn the children are receiving confident teaching and a broader curriculum.

In their responses to a written follow-up questionnaire presented after two years of implementing the National Curriculum, the proportion of headteachers reporting little or no impact on the learning of more able children remained unchanged compared with that after one year. The following comments indicated these headteachers' apparent satisfaction with this outcome:

> These pupils have adapted to the demands of the National Curriculum and have coped well with the programmes of study. They are capable of independent learning and progress at their own pace.

> Our work has not significantly altered and such children are still encouraged and stretched.

One headteacher went so far as to claim that these children coped easily with the demands of the National Curriculum.

As during the previous year only four headteachers referred to positive gains from the introduction of the National Curriculum for these children. Their comments were predominantly concerned with the curriculum planning benefits for the teacher which enabled them to plan more effectively in order to extend the learning of the more able children. No adverse effects were reported.

To sum up, as in the case of the class teachers, the headteachers' original predictions of mainly beneficial effects of the introduction of the National Curriculum appeared to have been borne out up to two years afterwards, at least in terms of their own perceptions, although fewer headteachers reported benefits compared with the number predicting them. The class teachers and headteachers reported similar kinds of benefits and very few teachers (and only one headteacher) reported any negative effects upon the more able learners.

Slower learners
The pattern of headteacher predictions about the likely impact of the National Curriculum upon the teaching of slower learning children, including those with special educational needs, was appreciably different from that reported above with regard to more able learners since a higher proportion predicted possible adverse consequences for these children. Approximately one-third of them expected the National Curriculum to have little or no impact, five predicted possible benefits and just over one-third predicted a negative impact due to the greater pressure to achieve which the National Curriculum was expected to exert upon slower learning children, coupled with reduced class teacher time to devote to supporting them. One headteacher felt that the practice of mixed ability teaching was now under threat.

The actual impact of the National Curriculum, as judged by the headteachers after one year, accorded with their predictions with regard to the different outcomes. Those teachers reporting little or no impact claimed that their slower learning pupils were continuing to work at their own pace and level and that the work was sufficiently differentiated to meet their learning needs. The few references to positive benefits stressed the breadth of the new curriculum, one teacher commenting that the National Curriculum would ensure that this group would have access to the whole curriculum. The reported negative effects, like the predictions, stressed the new pressures now placed on slower learning pupils, either directly or indirectly as a result of pressures upon their teachers. The following comments reflect the obvious concern of these particular headteachers about the dangers for these children:

> There is more pressure on teachers to get this group up to standard [for example, level 1] at least for the sake of the parents who will become more familiar with the levels.

> The National Curriculum has had a dramatic effect on them. The school can no longer give them the attention that they need. They are culturally deprived and just need the 'real basics'. Teachers are now under pressure to analyse what children are learning and when they review it and the children are not making great progress it is demoralizing for the whole staff. (Headteacher of a Social Priority Area school)

> These children don't have enough time to get through the tasks. Pressure of time creates disadvantages for slower learners.

> Failure could be reinforced earlier if the ethos of the school is wrong.

> They find it difficult to cope with the work and assimilate it in so many subjects.

One year later the pattern of the headteachers' responses to the same question in the written follow-up questionnaire was broadly similar to that reported after one year. Six headteachers judged that the National Curriculum had made little impact upon the slower learners. Two of the few headteachers reporting benefits referred to the greater effort and determination of their teachers to work harder with their slower learning pupils to enable them to reach the attainment targets, and one claimed that a far more structured approach to the teaching of these children had now been adopted. The description of negative outcomes once again referred to the pressure now being placed on these pupils to progress towards the attainment targets but, on this occasion, some headteachers expressed the view that insufficient time was now being spent upon the 'basic skills' of reading and number to meet these children's needs.

Differentiating the National Curriculum

These pupils are badly served by the demands of the National Curriculum as the time spent on the basic subjects has been reduced to fulfil the demands of a much more rigid curriculum.

One headteacher reported his staff's concern that children with difficulties in reading and number were being left behind, while another reported that the difference between the more able and the slower learning children was becoming more marked.

In summary it is clear that, for both class teachers and headteachers the number of reported adverse effects of the National Curriculum upon the teaching of the slower learning children exceeded that of reported benefits. The quality of these children's grasp of basic skills and concepts was seen to be threatened by the weight of the wider curriculum demands and the drive to work towards average levels of performance in the various attainment targets was putting undue pressure upon these children. Also the consequences of their failure to reach the expected target levels were likely to damage their self-esteem.

Chapter 6

The Teachers' Views on the Impact of the National Curriculum

In this chapter we look at the views of the teachers on various aspects of the National Curriculum in the light of their experience of implementing it over two years. The reponses of the Year 1 class teachers will be followed by those of the headteachers.

The Year 1 Class Teachers' Views

Problems in Delivering the National Curriculum

The Year 1 class teachers were asked whether they had experienced any particular problems or difficulties in implementing the National Curriculum during the first year (1989–90). All but seven teachers (twenty-six out of thirty-three) stated that they had done so. The most frequently mentioned problem was finding the time to meet the demands of the new curriculum in terms of its coverage (range of attainment targets) and the required assessment and record keeping, while at the same time keeping abreast of the statutory and non-statutory curriculum documents as they appeared. One teacher commented that much more time was needed for planning as there was so much to cover and, since she was not familiar with the documents she continually had to refer to them, which took up valuable teaching time. Several teachers referred to the problem of striking the right balance between teaching, assessment and recording. A different problem mentioned by a teacher in a school serving a disadvantaged area was that of getting poorly motivated learners to complete the prescribed work.

Several teachers expressed concern at the sheer scope of the new curriculum and felt that this increased coverage was being

The Teachers' Views

achieved by 'skimming the surface' at the expense of teaching in reasonable depth, or, in one teacher's words, the problem of 'fitting it all in knowing that justice is being done in each area'. Making an objective judgment of the breadth versus depth issue was difficult to do when one was engaged in ongoing teaching of the new curriculum according to another teacher.

The above problems were some of those actually experienced by the teachers during the first year of the implementation of the National Curriculum but, prior to this year (i.e. during the summer term 1989), the same teachers had been asked what problems they anticipated when implementing the National Curriculum in the coming school year. The anticipated and actual problems can therefore be compared. There is of course a danger in asking about anticipated problems, namely that the person asked will be predisposed to perceive subsequent problems in a self-justifying pattern. To counter the effects of such a possible bias it would be necessary to have, for comparison, a group of teachers who were not asked what, if any, problems they anticipated, but merely what, if any, problems they had actually experienced. However the inclusion of such a comparison group of teachers was not feasible in this study. In the event there were some differences in the nature of the problems reported and those anticipated which suggests that if there was a 'self-justifying' effect it did not operate strongly.

The number of teachers who anticipated some problems (twenty-seven out of thirty-three) was almost identical with the number subsequently reporting such problems. Amongst the anticipated problems, that of finding time to meet all of the demands of the National Curriculum was again prominent but, at this stage, the teachers saw these as focusing upon the difficulty of finding time to cope with the demands of assessment and record keeping, particularly in classes with a wide age or ability spread, including classes containing nursery-aged children. This particular concern was understandable given the relative lack of official information about the nature of the required assessments at that time. One teacher felt that she would need to be far more aware of the individual child in order to be able to assess and record his or her development and progress.

The fact that there were fewer specific references to actual, as opposed to anticipated, problems associated with assessment and record keeping might be taken to suggest that, on the whole, the Year 1 teachers coped better with these demands than they had anticipated, although it should be pointed out that, at this stage, the shools were not involved in the administration of the SATs. However an indication that such problems were still of concern to some of the teachers came from their responses to a question in the questionnaire completed by the teachers toward the end of the first year of implementation of the National Curriculum (that is, in 1990).

In this questionnaire the teachers were asked what problems they anticipated during the following year. While only eleven out of the thirty-three teachers responding expected any problems, most of those mentioned were again concerned with the management of time with particular regard to meeting assessment and record keeping requirements. One teacher put it as the problem of 'managing the time to do all that the government requires and to *teach* the children'. Concern was also expressed by a few teachers about achieving full curriculum coverage, particularly in the light of the introduction of some of the National Curriculum non-core subjects during the following year. The timing of the latter was commented on by some teachers, for example,

> It would have been nice to have had a year to reinforce the core subjects *before* the introduction of the foundation subjects.

The fact that only one-third of the teachers anticipated any problems during the second year of the National Curriculum might be taken as an indication that they were feeling more confident in their ability to meet its demands. (It also lends support to the view expressed earlier that the teachers' reported problems were not simply a reflection of the problems they anticipated.) Evidence for such a gain in the teachers' confidence also came in their responses to a question in the follow-up questionnaire which asked them to compare their current feelings about the National Curriculum with those approximately one year earlier.

The Teachers' Views

The majority of the teachers (twenty out of thirty-three) felt 'more happy' regarding the National Curriculum, with only eight teachers feeling unchanged in their views and two teachers feeling less happy than before. Their spontaneous comments on this question suggest the reasons for their generally more positive feelings. The fact that the teachers had by now had a year's experience of delivering the National Curriculum and were more familiar with the documents was clearly a major confidence building factor. There was a feeling amongst some teachers that their earlier fears had been unfounded, two of them commenting that it is the unknown which causes anxiety, and another stating that thinking about it is worse than doing it.

The experience of teaching the new curriculum had obviously helped them to come to terms with the practical demands of planning and timing. As one teacher put it,

> It's all more familiar after working with the documents for a year and knowing areas of weakness and the timing of the work. Even with the [forthcoming] introduction of the foundation subjects there is much less anxiety than this time last year.

Effect of the National Curriculum on the Teacher's Role, Methods of Teaching and Classroom Organization

Toward the end of the first year of the introduction of the National Curriculum the Year 1 teachers were asked at interview about its effects upon their role as class teachers and upon their methods of teaching and classroom organization. The same question was completed in the written follow-up questionnaire repeated approximately one year later. On both occasions the majority of teachers indicated that there had been significant changes in these respects but a minority (thirteen teachers each time) felt that their work had not changed in any significant way. On each occasion there was a mixture of positive and negative responses, with the latter being more numerous than the former.

On the positive side a few teachers commented that their planning was far more meticulous than previously because of the

National Curriculum. One said that she was experimenting with various teaching methods to accommodate the amount of work the National Curriculum requires and to execute it successfully to the benefit of all children. For another the National Curriculum had made her more aware of her role as class teacher in ensuring that the core subjects were not taught as separate subjects but were interrelated so that breadth, depth and relevance were demonstrated. The greater breadth of the new curriculum was reflected in the response of the teacher who said,

> It made me realize that I hadn't provided certain subjects in the past to the required depth and I have made a determined effort to include the subjects into my everyday teaching and to give children more opportunities for their own discoveries.

Another teacher commented that the National Curriculum had made her more aware of the importance of providing a structured, balanced form of learning with progression and continuity as a major factor.

Associated with this more detailed and careful planning was a greater degree of collaboration between teachers within a school, mentioned by some. These comments related more to curriculum planning than methods of teaching as such, about which there were relatively few statements, apart from a few references to the increased amount of group work amongst pupils taking place since the introduction of the National Curriculum.

On the negative side there were frequent references on both occasions to the increased pressure on class teachers resulting from the introduction of the National Curriculum and its associated assessment and record keeping requirements. In particular this pressure was perceived as stemming from the requirement that teachers should help all pupils to meet the full range of attainment targets at the appropriate levels. One teacher referred to the 'pressure to meet deadlines and to keep pushing the children forward even if they are not ready'. Another redefined her role as 'someone who has to teach the National Curriculum and balance time as best as possible to cover as many attainment targets as possible'. In contrast the teacher who stated that she

The Teachers' Views

found it 'a little difficult' to cover the attainment targets due to having a mixed class sounded only a mildly critical note.

The pressure brought on by the new demands for assessment and record keeping were reflected in comments such as the following:

> The role is far more demanding in the amount of record keeping which places increasing demands on the teacher's already overburdened workload. As a class teacher I am more restricted in my planning for the year with the National Curriculum and more time is spent recording assessments of children as 'proof' for any HMIs.

This pressure was felt by a number of teachers to extend into their domestic lives as indicated by comments such as

> There is more pressure outside of the classroom and in family life because of the time teachers need for all the paper work. The National Curriculum seems to be continually on one's mind. I never switch off from school.

For some teachers at least the increased pressures had detracted from their former enjoyment of their work, leading to responses such as

> The enjoyment of child based teaching has gone. We haven't time to spend on the things the children bring in. I feel bogged down with form filling and writing files and records. This gives less time for real teaching for which I was trained.

Another teacher commented that the pastoral role of the infant teacher had changed because there was now little time to listen to children's problems. A teacher who had been involved in the administration of SATs to Year 2 children saw herself as 'more of an assessor and examiner, a deliverer of the National Curriculum now, as opposed to a reactor to the needs and interests of children'.

Several teachers clearly regretted the constraints which the

The Impact of the National Curriculum

National Curriculum had placed upon their former flexibility in curriculum planning in reponse to children's spontaneous interests. As one put it

> The aims of the teacher to act as a catalyst and to encourage and show children how to learn and ask questions are restricted now because of the attainment targets I have to teach. Interesting opportunities are sometimes lost and not pursued because of the time element in which to achieve my attainment targets.

One teacher even felt that she was no longer in (curricular) control as the National Curriculum had taken control of her.

Even some of the teachers who felt that the introduction of the National Curriculum had not significantly affected their teaching role or methods acknowledged the restrictions now placed upon their planning freedom, for example:

> My methods haven't changed in respect of treating children according to their own individual needs but my scope has been restricted because of the statements of attainment I have to teach to now.

Not all of these teachers shared this feeling of restriction however, as exemplified in the response

> I have always taught cross-curricular, therefore the National Curriculum hasn't affected me greatly, only to increase record keeping. Even though the National Curriculum is subject based, with careful planning, the subjects can be brought together into cross-curricular work quite effectively.

Benefits and Disadvantages of the National Curriculum

In addition to the above questions asked at the 1989 and 1990 interviews the teachers were asked to state the benefits and disadvantages of the newly introduced curriculum. This question was repeated in the written follow-up questionnaire completed in 1991. Some of the response themes already noted appear again in the class teachers' responses to this question. On both occasions the majority of teachers listed both benefits and disadvantages, with only a handful noting either one or the other or neither. It is encouraging that around half of the teachers proposed curricular benefits of some kind. Some of these were associated with the wider curriculum content of the National Curriculum, particularly with regard to science and technology, and the wider range of activities engaged in by the children, including more practical work and more collaborative group work.

A number of teachers clearly felt that the National Curriculum provided a valuable planning framework which enabled them to see continuity and progression in each curriculum area and to plan in a more structured way than before. Typical comments in this respect were:

Progression is more evident to the teacher when planning work and this can only be of benefit to the children. We know where to go from stage to stage.

Also the planning framework provided by the statements of attainment and programmes of study was seen by some as an important guide in assessing children's progress, as reflected in the following comments:

There are far stricter guidelines to follow. It is easier to plan work and see where the children are. The assessments make you think about what you have done and where you are going.

The new National Curriculum assessments were seen by some teachers as providing a more precise measure of children's levels of attainment in the core subjects than hitherto, as exemplified in the comment, 'I am able to see exactly which stage each child is at in each curriculum area.' Some teachers felt that the planning and assessment framework provided by the National Curriculum enabled them to plan work more effectively to meet pupils' individual curricular needs. The benefits of the National Curriculum were felt by a number of teachers to apply particularly to more able children, for whom it was seen as offering considerable scope, for example by giving them a wider range of experiences and greater independence.

The disadvantages of the National Curriculum were perceived especially with regard to the pressures it put upon both teachers and children. Some teachers clearly felt themselves to be under strong pressure to maximize their children's progress towards the many attainment targets in the core subjects. This, in turn, raised anxieties in some teachers about the depth and quality of their teaching and also about the effects of the pressures they were putting on their pupils.

> As there are so many attainment targets to cover within the year I am finding myself having to skim the surface of some attainment targets rather than spending more time teaching them so that the children will achieve a better understanding. Young children are expected to reach a certain level of achievement at a certain date in the year and this shows little consideration of the fact that early development is along different paths and at different times, depending on the child's readiness in the different skills.

Slower pupils were felt by some teachers to be particularly vulnerable to the pressures exerted by the National Curriculum.

> Slower children may be pushed towards levels of attainment when they are not ready and I worry that if they fail to meet them this will be seen as a reflection of bad teaching.

In a similar vein another teacher, in a school serving a socially disadvantaged area, commented on 'the immense pressure to get poorly motivated children to a reasonable standard' and felt worried that the poor standard of their work might be interpreted as due to poor teaching on her part. Another, working in a similar school, commented on the difficulty of setting her children more science and practical tasks when they were unable to read.

The Teachers' Views

Regarding children's failure to reach particular attainment targets, two teachers raised the question of whether the work should be repeated until the children did understand it. Their concern appeared to be that slower children would suffer if the teacher forged ahead regardless of how quickly they grasped concepts.

Several teachers responded that the increased breadth of the curriculum would lead to insufficient time being spent on the 'basic skills' of reading, writing and number. A teacher working in a disadvantaged area school commented that her children needed constant practice on 'the basics' since many had no books or pencils at home, but the National Curriculum made no allowance for this. At least one teacher found that she could not hear children read on a daily basis, as before, but now only once a week.

Summary of the Class Teachers' Views

Most of the Year 1 class teachers in the study had experienced some problems in implementing the National Curriculum during the first year. The greatest concern was expressed about the sheer range of the attainment targets in the core subjects (those in the non-core subjects being still to come) and the fear that this increased curriculum coverage could only be achieved at the expense of the depth and quality of teaching and of increased pressure on the children, particularly the slower ones, to reach the desired attainment targets. Additionally some teachers regretted the perceived loss of flexibility in the infant curriculum which had hitherto allowed them to exploit children's spontaneous interests as they arose. The demands on the teacher's time and class management skills made by the new assessment and record keeping requirements were another focal point of concern, with some teachers feeling that such demands interfered with the 'real job' of teaching, making the teacher's role more stressful and less enjoyable than before.

Despite these strongly expressed concerns it was encouraging that many teachers appeared to have gained in confidence in their ability to implement the National Curriculum as a result of their first year's experience of teaching it and well over half of them felt 'somewhat happier' about the National Curriculum at the end of the second year of its implementation than during the first year. The greater breadth of the new curriculum and the fact that it provided a clear curriculum planning framework with built-in continuity and progression were perceived as positive gains by a number of teachers. Some teachers also reported that the introduction of the National Curriculum had led to a greater degree of collaboration and teamwork between teachers within their schools.

The Headteachers' Views

Problems in Delivering the Curriculum

The majority of headteachers (twenty out of twenty-six) had anticipated that their schools would experience some difficulties in implementing the National Curriculum during its first year. Nineteen out of twenty-four subsequently reported having experienced some problems when interviewed toward the end of that year. These problems were focused on the demands of assessment and record keeping, on the pressure on their staffs and upon the difficulties in obtaining adequate resources to support the new curriculum. Regarding assessment and record keeping, the relative lack of official guidance on what to assess and record and the time such processes would take, especially since teachers had no free periods, were particular worries. One headteacher wondered whether the class teacher had the necessary expertise to carry out the finely graded type of teacher assessment that he anticipated. The comment by another headteacher that assessment and record keeping were administrative rather than teaching functions echoed the views of some class teachers, presented earlier, who contrasted such functions with 'real teaching.'

In both years some headteachers clearly felt that their schools had been under considerable pressure to keep abreast of the National Curriculum documents as they appeared and to formulate their schools' curricular policies in the light of these, although such pressures may have eased somewhat after the first year. In contrast, a few headteachers felt that as a result of prior discussion and planning their schools had been well prepared to accommodate the new curricular demands. The increased workload of the class teacher was noted by some headteachers, one of whom commented upon the many hours of extra work involved and the consequent increase in teacher stress.

Regarding other problems, shortages of material resources, especially for the practical activities required by the new curriculum, worried some headteachers, as did the lack of books (especially for the non-core subjects), of library space and also space for storing materials. In at least one school, which served a disadvantaged area, these problems were compounded by that of vandalism. Some headteachers commented upon their teacher's relative lack of confidence to teach certain subjects such as science, technology and Welsh for which the need for further training was recognized. At least one headteacher saw it as part of her role to build the confidence of her staff to meet the new curricular demands.

The problems facing small rural schools were highlighted by a number of headteachers, due to the wide age and ability ranges that typified classes to be found there and the inevitable limitations within small staffs in the teacher expertise needed to cover all aspects of the curriculum. At least one headteacher working in such a school felt a sense of isolation in knowing what was going on in other schools and worried whether his school was working along the right lines in its attempts to implement the National Curriculum.

Effects of the National Curriculum on the Headteacher's Role

As with the class teachers, the headteachers were asked about the effects of the National Curriculum upon their professional role towards the end of each of the first two years of its implementation. The majority of headteachers felt that there had been some changes in their role, some of which were clearly regretted. Increased pressure in some form was noted by several headteachers although some of them commented that this was partly due to other coincidental developments, particularly the introduction of local management of schools (LMS). In the words of one headteacher,

> Pressures have increased considerably because of constant changes and demands in all directions. The introduction of the National Curriculum is only a small part of this.

The statutory responsibility which headteachers had acquired for the effective implementation of the new curriculum appeared to be a particular source of challenge and, in some cases, stress to them as the following quotation indicates:

> I feel more accountable for every aspect of my work, especially for the effective delivery of the curriculum. The constraints which can impede any progress in my work cause grave concern, especially if out of my control.

The need for headteachers and class teachers to share the responsibility for implementing the new curriculum was stressed by one headteacher as follows:

> They [headteachers] become leaders of teams and teachers need a different attitude to the headteacher as the National Curriculum is nationally prescribed and they cannot blame the headteacher for schemes of work. It has to work for the school and the staff have to pull together to make it work.

Associated with this increased sense of accountability was the perception by some headteachers of an increased demand upon them to support and sustain the confidence and ability of their staffs to meet the demands of the National Curriculum. As one headteacher put it

> The headteacher must give confidence to staff and boost their morale that they are on the right track and find relevant help for areas of weakness. This puts pressure on the headteacher who must know the National Curriculum in detail to reassure staff and keep up to date with changes in it.

Another headteacher felt that, although his views about education had not changed, his role had as a result of the National Curriculum and of LMS which had caused him worry and pressure to make his role effective. He now saw himself as a 'facilitator and motivator' to his staff in respect of the implementation of the National Curriculum.

Increased administrative duties concerned some of the headteachers as illustrated in the following examples:

> My role as headteacher has changed significantly over the last few years. I have less time to attend to curriculum matters because of administrative work and a great deal of curricular responsibility has been delegated.

> . . . a feeling that greater emphasis on administration such as form filling, record keeping and achieving goals is necessary rather than the previous philosophical approach where values held seem different from those current.

> My office has changed. We are no longer teachers but financiers, accountants and diplomats.

Associated with this increase in administration was a sense of regret, expressed by some headteachers about the reduced teaching contact that they now had with children. However, although many headteachers reported increased burdens and stress in their post-National Curriculum roles, not all of their comments were negative in tone. As mentioned earlier, six headteachers felt that there had been little or no change in their role. Another felt that although the National Curriculum appeared 'threatening and overwhelming', confidence to cope with it should grow in time.

Changes in Methods of Infant Class Teaching and Classroom Organization

At the end of the first and second years following the introduction of the National Curriculum about half of the headteachers felt that it had resulted in little change in the methods of teaching or classroom organization in their infant schools or departments. Of the changes reported by the remaining headteachers, the tighter structuring of classroom activities in order to work toward specific attainment targets received frequent mention. Like their class teacher colleagues, whose views were presented earlier, some headteachers regretted the relative loss of spontaneity of infant education. The loss of 'fun time' in the primary curriculum was regretted by another.

Associated with these changes was the reduced opportunity for play in Year 1 and Year 2 classes, which the headteacher of one of the schools serving a disadvantaged area saw as particularly regressive since 'many of our pupils do not know how to play usefully'. As regards teaching method the only change noted was the increased use of group work in the classroom, a trend also reported by the class teachers.

The headteachers were also asked to note whether the introduction of the National Curriculum had affected their schools in any other respect. The increased pressure on staff arising from a greater work load and increased responsibility were mentioned by several headteachers, one of whom commented graphically as follows:

> The National Curriculum has put tremendous demands on an already hard-working and conscientious staff. There never seem to be enough hours in the day and 'Adds hours' at the end of the day deliver the final killing blow.[1]

Another headteacher noted more discernible mood swings in her staff due to this pressure, adding that 'the children are often the saving grace'.

On the positive side, the increased need for coordinated planning prompted by the introduction of the National Curriculum led the staff to collaborate more closely than before according to several headteachers. One stated that it had helped staff to become more of a team, supporting and sharing with each other, thus creating continuity of planning. This planning framework had increased the sense of professionalism and confidence in some of the schools, as reflected in the following comments:

The National Curriculum has standardized what is being taught in schools and this gives teachers reassurance that they have been working in the right way.

The curriculum is far more organized. There is more whole school planning to accommodate sequential subjects like history and geography.

Benefits and Disadvantages of the National Curriculum

Like the Year 1 class teachers, the headteachers were asked to state what they perceived to be the benefits and disadvantages of the introduction of the National Curriculum toward the end of each of the first two years. As regards benefits only a handful of headteachers on each occasion appeared unable or unwilling to suggest any, although this did not necessarily reflect a negative view of the National Curriculum since, as mentioned earlier, some headteachers felt that the introduction of the National Curriculum had made relatively little difference to the curriculum they had already been offering. As one of these headteachers put it,

There is little benefit as such since the children are receiving much the same now as previously — perhaps science and experiments have increased and are more varied.

The benefits suggested by the majority related to curriculum planning, curriculum breadth and variety and to assessment and evaluation. Concerning the former, the National Curriculum had led to more thorough and coherent planning, with more continuity than before, according to a number of headteachers, as indicated in the following comments:

The National Curriculum helps teachers in their planning by giving targets to work towards.

What has to be done is stated clearly for staff to follow. Things which teachers have always done are now in black and white and in order. This is bound to be easier, particularly for the young inexperienced teachers.

Children follow a well defined programme of study in all curriculum areas. It has probably given a greater balance to the curriculum as staff plan to incorporate all strands of the National Curriculum in their lessons.

The broader curriculum and greater variety of curriculum activities such as practical work in mathematics, science and technology, were welcomed by several headteachers, as they had been by some of the class teachers. One headteacher commented that a wider range of subjects and approaches to learning were now available to children, who were more stimulated as a result.

Perceived positive aspects of the newly introduced methods of assessment and record keeping were identified by some headteachers as the following comments show:

Teachers can see how well they are doing. For the first time staff can actually state levels of attainment which they could not do before.

The National Curriculum gives a yardstick by which slower children can be measured to see how far behind they are.

Teachers can measure progress against specific objectives and statements with common criteria for all pupils.

The stated disadvantages of the National Curriculum fell mainly under the headings of increased pressure on teachers and children and reduced flexibility in curriculum planning. As with the benefits, a handful of headteachers on both occasions failed to state any disadvantages. The increased pressure upon school staffs was described in comments such as the following:

There is constant pressure to complete programmes of work across a wide range of subjects. Children are too young to be subjected to this pressure and meeting so many new subjects in a short space of time.

Such pressure was felt by some headteachers to be falling particularly on slower pupils, as illustrated in the following comment:

> There is no real disadvantage for bright pupils but I feel anxious for slower pupils and under-achievers. I feel there *may* be too much pressure too early on. Young children need time to play, socialize and mix and these aspects of the infant curriculum may suffer as a result of the National Curriculum, thus disadvantaging the children.

The increased pressure upon teachers already discussed was thought likely by some headteachers to have negative effects upon the children in time, for example,

> Teachers are over-worked and over-stressed and their low morale cannot be of help to the children. The intense pressure must be relaxed so that the true benefits of an exciting new curriculum can be realized.

Part of the pressure on teachers was judged by some headteachers to have resulted from too many curriculum changes at one time, threatening teachers' confidence and expertise.

The constraining effect of the National Curriculum on the primary teachers' traditional freedom and flexibility of curriculum planning was particularly mentioned by some headteachers in their responses to the follow-up questionnaire completed after the second year of implementation of the National Curriculum. This might reflect the cumulative impact of the introduction of the non-core subjects on top of the core subjects already in place. The sense of an overcrowded curriculum was conveyed in such comments as:

> There isn't enough time in the day to do everything required plus following a thematic approach. Teachers find themselves pulled in all directions, particularly with the humanities. A free interest based approach is impossible when targets have to be reached.

> The curriculum has been narrowed and there is a lack of spontaneity created by over-planning. It should be remembered that these children are only five!

Other disadvantages mentioned related to the reduction of teaching resulting from the demands of record keeping and assessment and the dilution of the curriculum at the expense of its greater breadth, a theme that emerged strongly in the class teachers' responses. The following list of disadvantages of the National Curriculum provided by one headteacher usefully summarizes the comments of many headteacher colleagues in the research sample:

- subjects overloaded with statements of attainment;
- too many attainment targets;
- little time for reflection and evaluation;
- record keeping is time consuming;
- the National Curriculum is subject based.

Toward the end of the first National Curriculum year the headteachers were asked to compare their feelings towards the National Curriculum with those expressed a year previously. Half of them (twelve) felt happier about its introduction than before, ten responded that their feelings were unchanged and two felt less happy. The stated reasons for feeling happier about the National Curriculum included the headteachers' perception of an increase in their class teachers' confidence in their approach to it and the realization that the new curriculum did not differ drastically from that which had operated prior to its introduction. The following comments illustrate these positive feelings:

> It is continuing good practice and making everyone better at planning the activities provided for the children.

> The staff realize that it's work they have been doing before in any case. The more familiar they become with the National Curriculum levels the easier it will be.

Such references to curriculum continuity need to be juxtaposed with both class teachers' and headteachers' comments reported

The Teachers' Views

earlier about the greater breadth and scope of the National Curriculum in relation to the schools' existing curricula, particularly with regard to science and technology.

The increased confidence amongst some school staffs appeared to stem partly from their perception of curriculum continuity just noted and also from their realization, based upon a year's experience, that they could meet the challenges posed. The following comments echo the views of some class teachers reported earlier:

> We are coming to terms with it. It's not as frightening as first appeared.

> We've met the challenges — the staff are much happier because of the self support system within the school.

Some of the headteachers whose feelings remained unchanged stressed the preparation that their schools had made for the introduction of the National Curriculum, as illustrated in comments such as,

> The school was quite well prepared last year and the National Curriculum has not made any dramatic difference to our way of working. The National Curriculum has been absorbed.

Several headteachers wanted to reserve judgment about the impact of the National Curriculum, given the relatively early stage of its implementation and their awareness that more work needed to be done on it by them.

The following two comments expressed the difficulty felt by some headteachers in making objective judgments about the quality of their school's implementation of the National Curriculum:

> It is hard to judge the school's delivery of the National Curriculum until it is reviewed by an outside body.

> It is difficult to be objective about your own school.

The Impact of the National Curriculum

Headteachers' Overall Views about the National Curriculum

In addition to stating the benefits and disadvantages of the National Curriculum, the headteachers (but not the class teachers) were asked for their overall comments on the effects of its introduction toward the end of the first and second years respectively. On both occasions, but particularly the later one, the negative comments tended to outweigh the more positive ones although this should not be interpreted as indicating a predominantly negative view towards the National Curriculum on the part of the headteachers (see Chapter 7). Predictably there was some overlap between their responses to the two different questions. Positive comments, such as the following, corresponded with some of the stated benefits of the National Curriculum in stressing the improved team work and collective planning by school staffs:

> A greater sharing is taking place of ideas, resources and talents.

> It has made teachers work as a team. Teachers are looking closely at what is being done in the classroom and their own method. It has helped the teachers to look more closely at individual children and to develop ways of observing children at work.

> Teachers are rising to the challenge. They *have* to work as a team and not as individuals as before.

Other positive comments made by the headteachers referred to the dedication of their staffs and to their own efforts to maintain their teachers' morale and positive attitudes in the face of the challenges they were facing:

> Infant staff have worked extremely hard to ensure the success of the introduction.

> We have tried to be positive — always looking on the bright side — morale must be kept high.

The Teachers' Views

Initially it affected the morale of teachers. Pressure of work and time left teachers thoroughly exhausted. I have committed staff who have always worked above and beyond what was expected of them.

Some of the negative comments centred upon the increased work load and pressure on teachers, particularly with regard to assessment and record keeping and echoed those reported earlier. One such reponse highlighted the particular pressure placed upon staff in small rural schools:

Because it is a small school there is too great a pressure and expectation on teaching staff in delivering the National Curriculum. They have to take on too many responsibilities which in a larger school would be spread around.

Other negative comments expressed strong disapproval of the rate of change imposed on schools by the introduction of the National Curriculum, particularly in conjunction with other changes stemming from the Education Reform Act. Amongst such changes the daunting effect that the sheer volume of documentation can have on teachers was clearly reflected in the following comment:

The rapid and ever increasing amounts of materials bombarding schools is leading teachers to become dispirited and tending not to read the plethora of written recommendations and instructions. Clearer guidelines, of which there appears to be a better appreciation at the Welsh Office, need to be issued to replace the piles of documents already issued so that they can be dumped.

In their responses to the follow-up questionnaire completed toward the end of the second National Curriculum year, a few headteachers expressed particular frustration at the further changes that had been made to attainment targets in the core subjects of maths, English and science and resented the lack of oppportunity for consolidation and long term planning that resulted from them:

The Impact of the National Curriculum

> The fact that the maths and science attainment targets are being reorganized confirms my view that the National Curriculum is being introduced in haste. More time in planning and introducing would provide a more solid foundation on which schools and teachers could build with confidence. A great deal of work in planning a suitable recording system in this school has been wasted effort in view of these changes.

> I think that everything has been rushed and we have been overwhelmed with new ideas too quickly. We have spent a lot of time working out our policies only to find that they are out of date as something else has taken their place. Changes are being made in maths, English and science again. This is very frustrating — things are far too unsettled.

Finally a number of critical comments referred to the rigidifying effect of the National Curriculum on curriculum planning stated earlier by some headteachers as a disadvantage of the National Curriculum. In particular its subject orientation was attacked, as in the following comments:

> A considerable amount of time, effort, sweat and tears has been put in to make the implementation of the National Curriculum work only to find that its subject based approach does not weld with the thematic approach. The subjects are overloaded and there is no perception of how the whole curriculum will fit together.

> I believe the National Curriculum has distinct benefits. Now it must be made to work. Every subject is overloaded. We must try to ensure that each subject does not become a separate entity.

Summary of the Headteachers' Views

The majority of headteachers reported that their schools had experienced some problems in implementing the National

Curriculum during the first two years, including increased pressure on class teachers to achieve the relevant attainment targets and to meet the demands of assessment and record keeping, and a shortage of the material resources needed. Like their class teacher colleagues most of them felt that their professional role had changed to some degree as a result of the introduction of the National Curriculum, coupled with other changes stemming from the ERA. Apart from a greater administrative workload the main changes were a sharper sense of professional accountability arising from the new legal responsibility for delivering the new curriculum, and a heightened awareness of their role in leading and supporting their staff and maintaining their confidence during a time of stress and challenge. Opinions were evenly divided about the impact of the National Curriculum on methods of teaching and organization in infant classrooms but those who felt there had been some change reported a tighter degree of structuring of classroom activities and reduced flexibility in curriculum planning resulting from the drive to meet the various attainment targets across the curriculum. The reduced opportunity for free play, particularly for disadvantaged children, was a strong concern of some headteachers.

The perceived benefits of the National Curriculum included better curriculum planning with greater continuity and progression than before and a broader, more varied curriculum and range of learning experiences. Disadvantages were felt to arise mainly from the increased pressure to achieve the relevant attainment targets which affected both teachers and children, particularly the slower learners who needed time to consolidate their learning. Nevertheless, as with the class teachers, half of the headteachers reported feeling happier about the National Curriculum one year after its introduction.

The headteachers' overall comments on the National Curriculum ranged from very positive to strongly negative. The favourable comments stressed the greater collaboration now taking place amongst teachers within their schools and the dedication and hard work of those teachers in trying to implement the National Curriculum effectively. On the negative side strong disapproval was expressed about the greatly increased workload and pressure on class teachers arising from the demands of the

National Curriculum, and also about the rapid pace at which it had been introduced at Key Stage 1. Particular frustration was expressed at the sheer weight of documentation and the fact that changes were already being made to some of the core subject attainment targets so soon after their introduction. A further criticism of some headteachers concerned the over-loaded nature of the new curriculum, both within and across subjects.

Overall the views of the headteachers and Year 1 class teachers regarding the positive and negative features of the National Curriculum broadly corresponded, with differences in emphasis which appeared to reflect the differences in their respective roles. Both groups felt that it provided a helpful planning framework, with clear aims and objectives, but strongly regretted the pressure which it engendered toward meeting the wide range of attainment targets and the consequent loss of flexibility and spontaneity in curriculum planning.

In this chapter the spontaneous views of the headteachers and class teachers towards the National Curriculum, based upon two years' experience of implementing it, have been presented. In the following chapter the overall attitudes of the teachers towards the National Curriculum are examined, using a specially devised attitude measurement scale. While the content of that scale was somewhat different from that of the questions asked in the teacher interviews, some comparisons between the results of the two forms of enquiry will be made.

Note

1 The term 'Adds hours' is a local one referring to the statutory non-teaching contact time which all teachers are now required to spend as part of their contracts.

Chapter 7

Teachers' Attitudes to the National Curriculum

In this chapter we explore the attitudes and views of the teachers towards the National Curriculum using a specially designed attitude scale. This enabled us to compare the attitudes of the headteachers and Year 1 class teachers on three occasions, to see if they showed any significant changes over the three years of the study. The three occasions were approximately one year before the introduction of the National Curriculum (1989) and towards the end of the first and second years following its introduction (1990 and 1991).

An attitude can be defined as the organization of a person's psychological processes with respect to some aspect of the world which she or he distinguished from other aspects. These processes include thoughts and beliefs (cognitive processes), feelings (affective processes) and dispositions to behave in certain ways toward the object of the attitude (conative processes). Attitudes are learned and modified as the result of experience, often incidentally rather than systematically, and some are significantly related to an individual's personality, particularly her or his fundamental values and motives. Although an attitude will predispose us to behave in a certain way towards its object, our behaviour in a specific, real life situation will be subject to other important influences. This means that we cannot predict precisely how a given individual will behave in a particular context simply from a knowledge of her or his attitudes. In the case of teachers, therefore, even if we can accurately measure their attitudes to the National Curriculum we cannot assume that they will directly act out their beliefs toward it in the classroom since their behaviour will also be subject to other powerful influences, including the expectations of others. Even so it is important to try to measure teachers' attitudes to a reform as fundamental as the National Curriculum since they have a statutory commitment to its successful implementation and that is likely to be helped by positive attitudes and hindered by negative ones.

The written attitude scale devised for this study comprised fourteen statements about the National Curriculum, seven positive and seven negative, which the teachers were asked to respond to using a five-point scale ranging from 'strongly agree', through 'uncertain', to 'strongly disagree' (see Appendix 1). (Technical details about the scale can be found in Cox *et al.*, 1991). The selection of statements for the scale was made from a reading of the current educational press and from discussions with teachers at INSET and other meetings. The scale was piloted in two primary schools not included in the study sample. For the purpose of calculating a total attitude scale score, only ten of the fourteen items were used since, for the remaining four items it was found that the teachers' scores on those items showed little relationship to their total scores derived from all items in the scale. (The four items omitted from the total attitude scale score were items numbered 1, 2, 11 and 12 respectively.) However these four items were retained for the item by item analysis of results presented later in this chapter. Since the scores for each of the items ranged from 1 to 5 (i.e. from 'strongly disagree' to 'strongly agree' in the case of positively worded items and the reverse for negatively worded items) the minimum and maximum scale total scores were 10 and 50 respectively, with an arithmetical mid-point or 30.

The attitude scale was completed in writing by the teachers immediately prior to their interviews in 1989 and 1990 and as part of the written follow-up study carried out in 1991. Thus we obtained a measure of their attitudes to the National Curriculum approximately one year before its introduction and toward the end of the first and second years following that. We can therefore compare the results for each year to see if there are any significant changes over the study period. Before doing that, however, we will present the results for each year separately.

Year By Year Results

The distribution of the teachers' total attitude scale scores for each of the three years are shown in Figures 1 to 3 in which we have combined the scores of the headteachers and class teachers since they were found not to differ significantly (see Appendix 2, Table A.1 for the mean scale scores for headteachers and class teachers on each occasion). It is clear that in each year there is a wide spread of attitude scores ranging from strongly negative to strongly positive but on each occasion the scores tend to cluster around the arithmetical scale mean of 30.

While it is tempting to regard the middle of the score range on this scale as reflecting a neutral or moderate overall attitude toward the National Curriculum, one must be cautious in making such an interpretation because of the nature of the type of attitude scale used. Thus, in some cases, the total scores in the middle range may have resulted from a combination of both positive and negative scores on the various scale items, but in other cases the same total scores could have resulted from a high proportion of 'neutral' responses, that is, scoring 3 in the response scale. Thus the same middle range scores could reflect a consistently moderate or neutral attitude toward the National Curriculum, or, in contrast, an inconsistent attitude in which positive and negative views cancel each other out. However the more extreme total attitude scale scores are easier to interpret since they are likely to reflect the respondents' stronger, more consistent views. While it is encouraging to infer from Figures 1 to 3 that some of the sample teachers had strongly positive overall attitudes to the National Curriculum, it is somewhat alarming that there are other teachers whose overall attitudes appear to be strongly negative, even though, as we pointed out earlier in this chapter, we must not assume a direct link between a teacher's attitude and his or her classroom behaviour.

Trends in the Teachers' Attitudes over Time

It can be seen from Figures 1 to 3 that, while the attitude score distributions for each of the three years show a wide spread around the scale mean, those for 1990 and 1991 show a bias toward the

The Impact of the National Curriculum

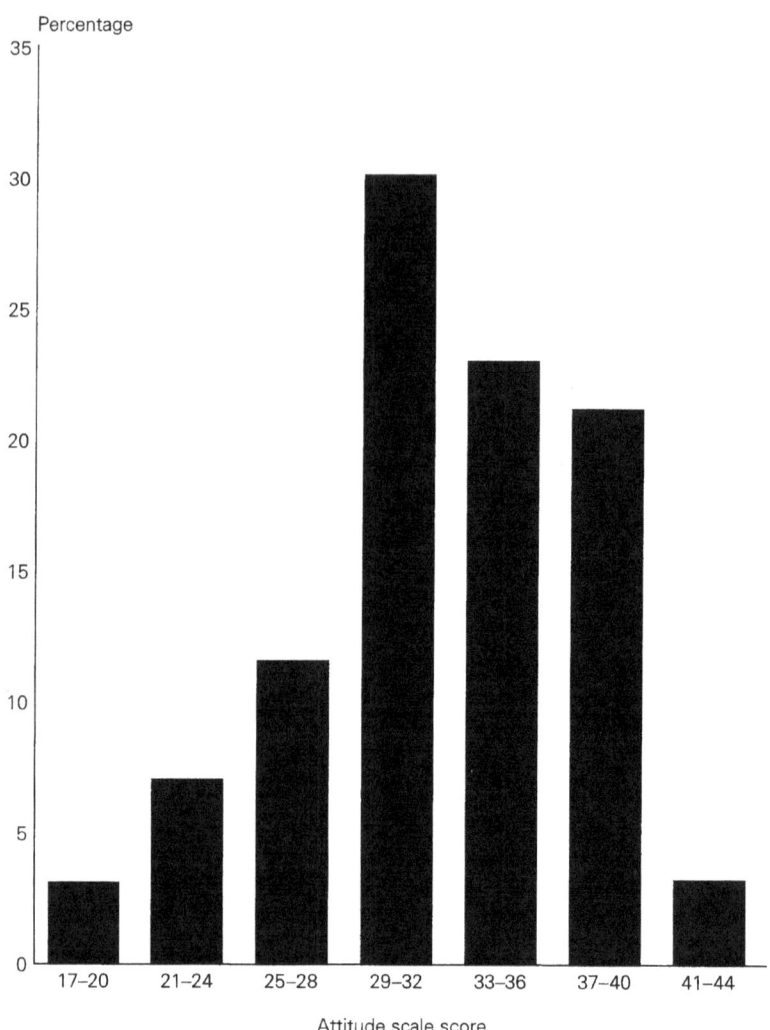

Figure 1   Teachers' attitude scale scores in 1989
Note: N = 57; Mean = 32.00

negative end of the score range. Statistical testing confirmed that the teachers' mean scores for each of those years were significantly lower than that for 1989, although there was no significant difference between the means for 1990 and 1991 (see Appendix 2, Table A.2.) Since the composition of the sample of Year 1 class teachers had changed somewhat during the three years

Attitudes to the National Curriculum

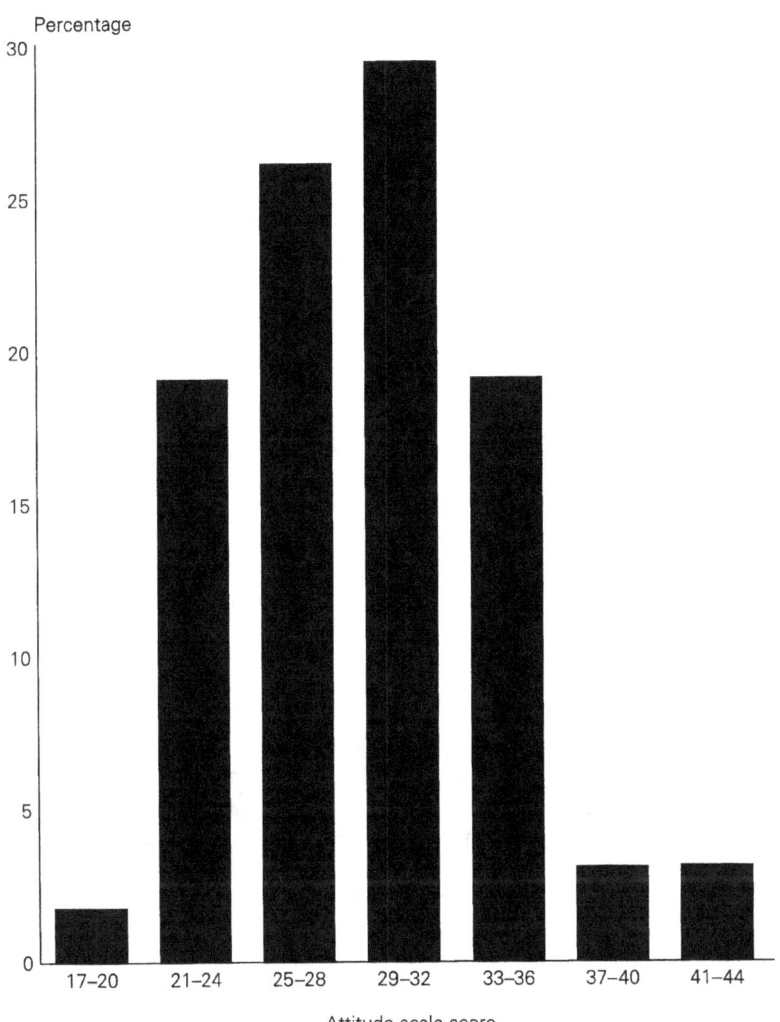

Figure 2   Teachers' attitude scale scores in 1990
Note: N = 58; Mean = 29.33

of the study, we must be cautious about attributing this downward trend in the mean scores to a 'hardening' of teachers' attitudes to the National Curriculum. (The composition of the headteachers' sample remained stable over the three years, apart from minor changes.) In order to made a strictly fair comparison between the teachers' year to year scores it is necessary to identify those teachers

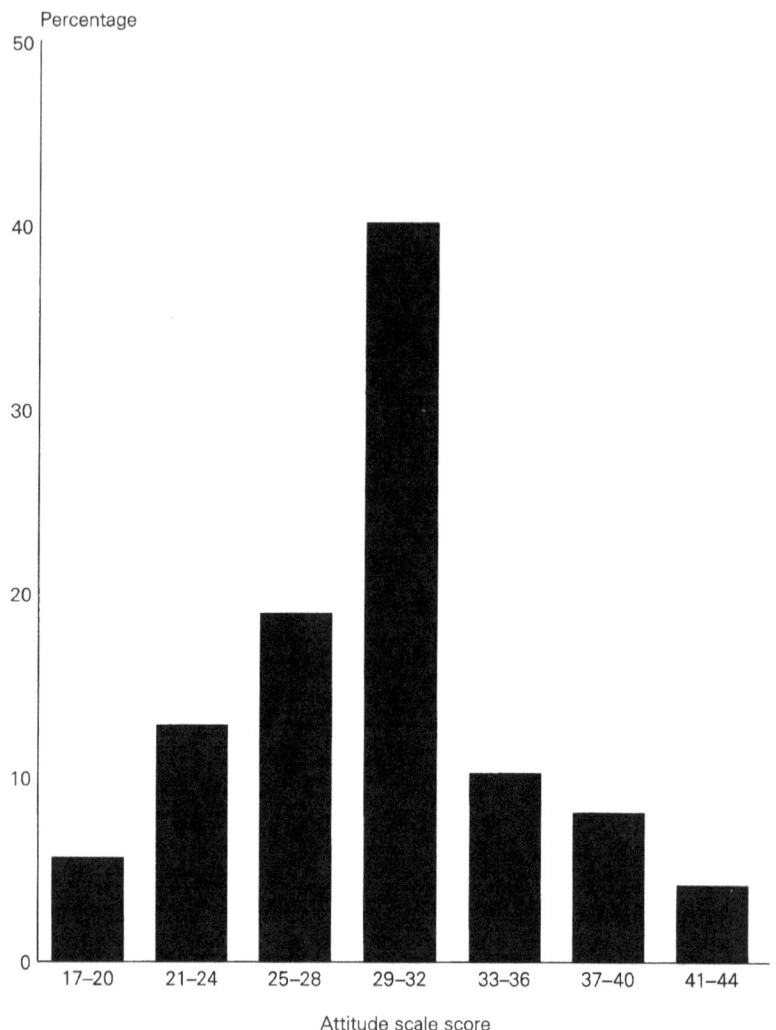

Figure 3   Teachers' attitude scale scores in 1991
Note: N = 52; Mean = 29.58

who responded to all three attitude questionnaires. This 'core sample' comprised thirty-five teachers, made up of twenty-one headteachers and fourteen Year 1 class teachers. The total attitude scale score distributions for this sample were plotted and were found to be very similar to those of the full sample and also to show the same negative trend over the three occasions (see

Attitudes to the National Curriculum

Appendix 2, Figures A.1 to A.3). Moreover the same pattern of between group differences emerged from the statistical testing as for the total sample. We can state with confidence then that, as a group, the teachers in this study appeared to become more negative in their overall attitudes toward the National Curriculum during the first two years of its implementation. We must emphasize though that this shift is a limited one for the teachers' attitude scores remained widely distributed about the mean on each occasion and at no time became predominantly negative.

One might expect this apparently negative shift in the teachers' attitudes to the National Curriculum to be reflected in their spontaneously expressed views reported in the previous chapter. In fact there is conflicting support for, on the one hand, at least half of the class teachers and headteachers judged that they felt happier about the National Curriculum one year after its implementation, but, on the other hand, negative views about the National Curriculum expressed by the headteachers in each of the first two years after its introduction tended to outweigh the more positive views, as did those of the class teachers regarding the impact of the National Curriculum upon their professional role. Since the attitude scale was made up of fourteen separate items it is worth examining the teachers' responses to each of these on each occasion to see if they can tell us something about the nature of the negative shift in the teachers' overall attitudes. For this analysis all fourteen of the attitude scale items will be used, not only the ten items used to compute the total attitude scale scores.

The full sample teachers' responses to each of the fourteen items of the attitude scale are shown in Table 8, from which we can identify those items where there appears to be a trend in the teachers' response patterns over the three occasions, either in the positive or the negative direction. Amongst the ten items which were used to compute the total attitude scale score there appears to be a negative shift in the response pattern over time for seven items (numbers 3, 5, 6, 7, 8, 9, and 10), with a similar shift for two of the four items not contributing to the total attitude scale score (numbers 2 and 12). In view of the changes in the composition of the teachers' sample over the study period mentioned earlier the responses of the 'core sample' of thirty-five teachers were also examined and these showed a similar negative shift on the same items as in the full sample.[1] Since the 'core sample' provides a more reliable guide to trends in the teachers' responses over time the following results are drawn from that sample only.

Of the items in which a statistically significant negative shift occurred two were concerned with National Curriculum assessment and reporting. In 1991, compared with 1989, more teachers endorsed the view that the formal assessment of attainment targets at age seven is too early and educationally unsound (item 10) and fewer endorsed the view that the SATs of the National Curriculum are essential to back up the teachers' own assessments (item 12). On the other items concerned with this topic the negative trends fell short of statistical significance. Two other scale items showed a statistically significant negative trend. First more teachers in 1991 agreed with the view that the National Curriculum posed a serious threat to cross-curricular (project) work because of its subject emphasis (item 2). Second fewer teachers in 1991 than in 1989 endorsed the view that the National Curriculum is broad, balanced and relevant to children's needs (item 9). There were no significant changes in the positive direction although there was a slight trend for more teachers in 1991 than in 1989 to disagree with the view that the introduction of the National Curriculum would lead to a concentration on 'the basics' (item 11).

A direct comparison between the teachers' views on the specific items of the attitude scale and their views expressed at interview is not possible since the questions guiding the latter were more concerned with the impact of the introduction of the National Curriculum, including its formal assessments, upon the teachers' professional role and methods rather than with its educational merits *per se*, although the latter sometimes received mention in the teachers' responses to the more open-ended questions. However the increased concern about the possible threat posed by the National Curriculum to cross-curricular work shown by the teachers in their responses to item 2 of the attitude scale was certainly reflected in the spontaneous comments of some of the teachers at interview.

On balance the evidence reported above indicates that, as a

Attitudes to the National Curriculum

group, the teachers in the sample became somewhat more negative in their attitudes to the National Curriculum, particularly with regard to the educational consequences of formal assessment. However this should not be taken to imply that their attitudes to the new curriculum were wholly negative for this was certainly not the case. Reference back to Table 8 shows that on some of the attitude scale items not concerned with formal assessment the majority (over 50 per cent) of teachers showed a positive view on each occasion. Thus, in each year, around 80 per cent of teachers welcomed the fact that the National Curriculum allowed them to decide how to achieve its aims (item 4), over 70 per cent disagreed with the view that the National Curriculum would mean a concentration on the 'basics' (item 11), and nearly 60 per cent disagreed with the view that the National Curriculum would seriously deprive the class teacher of professional freedom and scope for initiative (item 6). Finally, in both 1989 and 1990, over half of the teachers rejected the view that the National Curriculum was a backward educational move (item 13).

One might expect that as teachers gained experience in implementing the new curriculum they would become more definite in their views about it and that this would be reflected in fewer of them using the 'uncertain' response when completing the attitude scale subsequent to its first administration. From Table 8 it can be seen that there is indeed a trend for the percentage of respondents using this category to diminish between 1989 and 1991, although not between 1989 and 1990. This trend proved to be statistically significant for the full sample, but not for the 'core sample' although the latter teachers showed a similar downward trend in their use of this category. Two of the scale items showing a marked reduction in the proportion of uncertain responses were concerned with the formal assessment of children's attainments (items 10 and 12), which is consistent with the trend already reported for the teachers to become more negative in their views on this topic. On these particular questions the teachers' views certainly appeared to be crystallizing.

There were, however, three scale items where the proportion of teachers expressing uncertainty remained relatively high, i.e., over 25 per cent on all three occasions. These were item 9,

The Impact of the National Curriculum

Table 8 Teachers' views on the National Curriculum over three years

Attitude Scale Item	Date	Percentage Responding				
		strongly agree	agree	uncertain	disagree	strongly disagree
1 We will find the NC helpful because it tells us what to teach and when.	1989 1990 1991	3 0 4	39 41 40	26 26 17	23 31 36	9 2 2
2 The NC poses a serious threat to cross-curricular (project) work because of its subject emphasis.	1989 1990 1991	5 5 15	16 29 33	17 17 15	44 45 36	17 3 0
3 The NC will force teachers to concentrate on teaching those skills/attitudes that are most easily measured at the expense of those that are less easy to assess.	1989 1990 1991	2 3 6	26 48 52	23 29 21	39 17 21	10 2 0
4 I welcome the fact that the NC still allows us to decide how to achieve its aims.	1989 1990 1991	28 29 17	51 50 67	12 15 6	7 5 8	2 0 2
5 The reporting of pupils' performance will mean that teachers will not be able to get away with poor teaching.	1989 1990 1991	5 0 4	35 15 13	21 36 23	32 34 48	7 14 11
6 The NC will seriously deprive the class teacher of professional freedom and scope for initiative.	1989 1990 1991	3 3 4	16 22 25	17 15 13	53 52 52	10 7 6
7 The formal assessment of children at age 7 will have a narrowing effect on the primary (infant) curriculum.	1989 1990 1991	16 15 11	26 50 48	25 21 21	32 10 17	2 3 2

Attitudes to the National Curriculum

	Year					
8	The NC assessments will be helpful in backing up our judgments when discussing pupils with parents.	1989 1990 1991	7 2 6	72 52 52	10 24 17	10 22 25	0 0 0
9	The NC is broad, balanced and relevant to children's needs.	1989 1990 1991	5 2 0	49 34 38	39 41 40	7 22 19	0 0 2
10	The formal assessment of attainment targets at age 7 is too early and educationally unsound.	1989 1990 1991	32 36 35	23 38 38	30 15 17	16 7 8	0 3 2
11	The introduction of the NC means that we can concentrate on the basics and forget about the airy fairy subjects that have crept into primary education.	1989 1990 1991	2 0 2	2 5 2	23 5 10	39 62 56	35 28 31
12	The standard assessment tasks (SATs) of the NC are essential to back up the teachers' own assessments.	1989 1990 1991	0 0 0	51 15 6	39 38 15	7 34 58	3 12 21
13	The introduction of the NC is a backward move educationally.	1989 1990 1991	3 5 2	7 14 15	39 43 27	51 36 52	0 2 4
14	The introduction of the NC means that all pupils will get the same breadth and depth of curriculum regardless of which school they attend.	1989 1990 1991	2 2 2	40 28 27	26 26 29	30 29 35	2 15 8

Note: N = 57 (1989), 58 (1990) and 52 (1991)

stating that the National Curriculum was broad, balanced and relevant to children's needs, item 13, stating that the National Curriculum was a backward move educationally and item 14, stating that under the National Curriculum all pupils would get the same breadth and depth of the curriculum regardless of which schools they attended.

One can understand that some teachers might consider that two years is not long enough to decide whether the introduction of the National Curriculum really is a backward educational move. This relatively short time scale may also explain why a substantial proportion of them were still undecided about whether the new curriculum was broad, balanced and relevant to children's educational needs, or whether pupils were likely to gain its full curricular benefits regardless of which schools they attended. During the period of the study, the non-core subjects of, history, geography, music, technology, physical education and (in Wales) Welsh were successively introduced and the teachers were still in the very early stages of incorporating the new programmes of study into their curricula and teaching methods. Some teachers' spontaneous comments reported in the previous chapter indicated that they appreciated the scope and breadth of the full new curriculum but felt strong anxieties about the consequent danger of superficiality in the teaching of it.

Summary

In each of the three years when their attitudes were measured the teachers (headteachers and class teachers combined) showed a wide range of attitudes to the National Curriculum, ranging from the strongly positive to the strongly negative, with the majority of teachers lying between those extremes. There was a strong tendency for the teachers' attitudes to become less positive during the three years of the study, particularly with regard to the formal assessment of children's attainments. In addition the proportion of teachers regarding the National Curriculum as a serious threat to cross-curricular teaching significantly increased during this period. Associated with this pattern was a clear trend towards greater certainty amongst the teachers in their responses to the scale items, with the exception of three items. This apparently negative shift in attitudes towards the National Curriculum appeared to conflict with the finding reported in the previous chapter that at least half of the teachers reported feeling happier about the introduction of the National Curriculum in the second year of the enquiry but this could be due to the fact that the attitude scale addressed some educational issues not covered in the teachers' questionnaires. Despite this negative trend in overall attitudes the majority of teachers continued to express positive views regarding some aspects of the National Curriculum, agreeing that it provided a useful planning framework which still allowed them scope for professional initiative and they strongly rejected the view that the introduction of the National Curriculum would lead to an over-concentration on 'the basics'.

Note

1   In the full teachers' sample only items 2, 5, 8, and 12 showed a statistically significant negative shift when tested by the Chi-squared technique (1989 vs 1991). In the core sample only items 2, 5, 9, 10 and 12 showed a significant difference.

Chapter 8

Summary, Discussion and Conclusions

The following is a summary of the main findings of the study. These will then be discussed in relation to the findings of other relevant National Curriculum studies and reports from HMI and government agencies, with the exception of the findings concerning the education of under-5-year-old children, and the education of slower learning and socially disadvantaged children which will be discussed in Chapters 10 and 11 respectively.

1. In each of the three years of the study the headteachers and class teachers combined showed a wide range of measured attitudes towards the National Curriculum ranging from strongly positive to strongly negative but with the majority lying within these extremes. There was a strong tendency for the teachers' overall attitudes to become somewhat less positive during the first two years of the implementation of the National Curriculum than in the year prior to its introduction. This trend stemmed mainly from those items in the attitude scale which were concerned with the formal assessment of children's attainments. On the remaining items of the scale the majority of teachers responded positively on each of the three occasions when they completed the scale.
2. While there was recognition of the breadth and variety of the National Curriculum many teachers expressed concern about the sheer number of attainment targets and statements of attainment to be covered in the core subjects and felt that this wider curriculum coverage could only be achieved at the expense of the depth and quality of children's learning in these subjects.
3. Many class teachers, supported by their headteachers,

Summary, Discussion and Conclusions

expressed serious concern about the heavy demands upon their time and class management skills made by the new assessment and record keeping requirements which were felt by some teachers to reduce the time available actually to teach their pupils the new curriculum.

4   Many headteachers expressed strong disapproval about the greatly increased workload and pressures upon their class teachers arising from the demands of the National Curriculum and the rapid pace of its introduction at Key Stage 1. Particular frustration was expressed at the fact that changes had already been made to some core subject attainment targets and programmes of study soon after their introduction.

5   Despite the pressures exerted on them by the demands of the National Curriculum many teachers appeared to gain in confidence in their ability to meet these demands during the first year of its implementation. This was coupled with the recognition, by both class teachers and headteachers, of the fact that the National Curriculum provided a clear curriculum planning framework with built-in continuity and progression.

6   Headteachers reported feeling a sharper sense of professional accountability arising from their schools' responsibility to implement the new curriculum and a heightened awareness of their role in leading and supporting their staff in this process and in maintaining their morale during a period of stress and change.

7   There was a fairly even split amongst the headteachers in their responses to the question of whether the introduction of the National Curriculum had made an impact upon the methods of classroom organization and teaching at the infant stage. The view that the impact had been slight contrasted with reports of a tighter structuring of classroom activities, reduced flexibility in curriculum planning and a greater degree of collective staff planning and collaboration than previously.

8   In some classrooms the introduction of the National Curriculum appeared to reduce the scope for Year 1 teachers to engage in their children's free play activities,

although this trend was not strong when the amounts of free play time were compared in 1989 and 1990 in the teachers' sample as a whole. This was a source of concern to those teachers reporting such a reduction, especially with regard to slower learning children and those from socially disadvantaged backgrounds since free play activities were seen as providing the vital foundation for the development of these children's language, cognitive and social development.

9 Headteachers were divided in their views about the consequences of the introduction of the National Curriculum for the teaching of under-5-year-old children (including those in Year 1 classes). Some appeared to view the 'pre-5' curriculum in terms of preparing children for Key Stage 1 work and welcomed the opportunity to impose a firmer structure upon it than before. Others, however, expressed concern at what they saw to be the premature introduction of very young children to more formal National Curriculum-led teaching and stressed the importance of preserving the distinctive child centred character of early years education. The views of the latter were strongly supported by those of a group of infant teachers, drawn from several LEAs in the region who were invited to state their views on this question at an INSET seminar held after the completion of the study.

10 The majority of head and class teachers judged that the National Curriculum had made no major impact upon the teaching of more able pupils, claiming that these children continued to work at their own individual rates and levels and that they had been fully extended in their learning prior to the introduction of the National Curriculum. Where teachers did report some impact of the new curriculum upon these children's quality of learning only benefits were mentioned.

11 A substantial proportion of teachers reported that the introduction of the National Curriculum had put greater pressure upon slower learning children in order to reach the appropriate attainment targets. There was concern that the quality and depth of such children's learning

Summary, Discussion and Conclusions

might suffer as the result of this pressure. Some teachers also voiced the concern that an early and public failure of certain children to reach the attainment targets would have a damaging effect upon their motivation and self-esteem. A further worry was expressed that teachers would be unable to spend sufficient time in teaching these children the basic skills because of the wider curricular demands of the National Curriculum. Some class teachers themselves felt under pressure in their efforts to help slower learning children to reach the prescribed attainment levels.

12 Teachers' perceived needs for INSET and their confidence in being able to deliver the National Curriculum varied during the study. Initially their concerns focused on assessment and record keeping but, after relevant INSET, they felt better prepared in this regard. As new subject orders became available teachers looked for appropriate INSET focusing on the teaching of non-core subjects.

13 Over the study period both headteachers and class teachers perceived a change in the status and nature of the topic or cross-curricular approach to teaching. Topics became more focused, with a trend towards science, and the choice of topics appeared to be constrained by the emphasis upon whole school planning. Class teachers expressed diverse views about the suitability of a cross-curricular approach to the teaching of the National Curriculum, some considering that it was the only way to cover its breadth, while others thought that it would be impossible to cover the whole of the National Curriculum in this way. However, amongst the headteachers there was an increasing acknowledgment that discrete subject teaching would have a place in the teaching of the National Curriculum.

14 Anxieties about assessment and record keeping were expressed throughout the period of the study. After relevant INSET, however, teachers felt better prepared to undertake these activities; they then began to see the need for added resources, time and classroom help in order to

be able to carry out the procedures. Teachers also reported that it was in the area of assessment and record keeping that most change had taken place.

Discussion

Up to this point we have simply presented the findings of our study largely without comment and have tried faithfully to reflect the views of the teachers in our sample, based upon their experience of implementing the National Curriculum over two years. It is now necessary to examine these findings from the wider perspective of the outcome of other contemporaneous research studies and the literature on educational theory and practice.

The Research Background

We must first of all stress that our sample of teachers and primary schools was drawn from just one LEA in South Wales and involved only Year 1 class teachers and headteachers. While we are confident that the sample of schools was representative of primary schools in this particular LEA we cannot claim that it was equally representative of primary schools across England and Wales nationally. Moreover the study focused upon the implementation of the National Curriculum at Key Stage 1 only and in particular in Year 1. We must therefore relate our findings to those emerging from other studies which were somewhat wider in their scope and were based upon samples which may be more representative nationally.

For this purpose our main data sources were two ongoing large scale research studies of the impact of the National Curriculum on primary schools and teachers and also reports issued by various government-funded agencies such as Her Majesty's Inspectorate (HMI), now the Office for Standards in Education (OFSTED), the National Curriculum Council (NCC), and the Curriculum Council for Wales (CCW). The latter reports provide empirical data concerning the implementation of the National Curriculum at Key Stages 1 and 2 based upon HMI and

Summary, Discussion and Conclusions

OFSTED surveys and school inspections, as well as the results from specially convened teachers' conferences and from other consultation exercises directed at schools and LEAs.

The first large scale research project is entitled 'Primary Assessment Curriculum and Experience' (PACE) and is centred at the Universities of Bristol and of the West of England. It was based upon a sample of forty-eight primary and infant schools drawn from eight LEAs in England and Wales. Its overall aim was to evaluate the impact of the National Curriculum upon infant children and their teachers. Data were gathered from two rounds of structured interviews with 150 headteachers and infant teachers, the first of which was carried out in 1990, shortly after the introduction of the National Curriculum at Key Stage 1. The second round of interviews was carried out in 1992. In addition the research team made direct classroom observations of teachers and pupils working in a sub-sample of project schools.

The second major study was carried out at the University of Exeter under the title of the Leverhulme Primary Project (LPP). As part of this wide ranging study a written questionnaire survey of the views of 901 teachers from 152 primary schools in England and Wales was carried out in 1989. This sample was judged to be a nationally representative one since it closely matched the distribution of primary schools in England and Wales according to size and region. (see Wragg et al., 1989). This study was followed by a more recent survey of teachers from a representative sample of 131 primary schools, some of which had participated in the original survey, using a modified version of the original postal questionnaire which included a section addressed specifically to teachers of Key Stage 1 children.

Teachers' Overall Response to the National Curriculum

One of the main findings of our study was that, in terms of their measured attitudes, the headteachers and Year 1 class teachers in the sample appeared to be predominantly positive toward the National Curriculum in principle, although they were seriously concerned about aspects of the formal assessment of young children's attainments. This finding is very strongly supported by those from the PACE and Leverhulme studies respectively (Osborn and Pollard, 1991; Bennett et al., 1992). It was also strongly backed up by the reported observations of HMI and other government appointed agencies in the report by the Office for Standards in Education (OFSTED) published in 1993a. Indeed we have not encountered any publication which claims that primary teachers are opposed to the National Curriculum *in principle*.

Similarly our finding that the teachers welcomed the planning framework offered by the National Curriculum, with its built in progression is supported by the results of other studies. The PACE project reported that most of the teachers in the study welcomed at least some aspects of the National Curriculum, particularly the curriculum clarification and focus it provided (Osborn and Broadfoot, 1991; Osborn et al., 1993), and the Leverhulme Project found that the primary teachers were using the National Curriculum widely as a planning framework, through its statements of attainment and programmes of study (Bennett et al., 1992). This is perhaps the most encouraging finding from the various studies which suggests that, despite being imposed upon teachers and schools by government decree, the National Curriculum has met a long standing need for detailed curriculum guidance.

The Manageability of the National Curriculum

Despite their positive acceptance of the National Curriculum in principle, the teachers in our study expressed two very serious concerns about its implementation in practice. The first of these was about the sheer scale of curricular prescription in terms of the number of attainment targets and statements of attainment which they saw as a threat to the quality of the children's learning. This concern was echoed by HMI in their published response to the 'three wise men' consultative document sent to all primary schools and LEAs in England (Alexander et al., 1992). In their report (OFSTED, 1993a) HMI state that, while expressing strong support for the National Curriculum in principle and acknowledging the better balance and greater breadth which it had brought

Summary, Discussion and Conclusions

to children's educational experience, teachers in England showed strong concern over its manageability with regard to capacity of primary schools to teach all subjects in the necessary depth. Manageability was seen as a particular problem at Key Stage 1 where the fundamental and time-consuming introduction of young children to the learning of literacy and numeracy had to be undertaken together with the work on the full range of the National Curriculum core and non-core subjects. The report explicitly warned that if schools were overstretched to provide the National Curriculum then the depth of children's learning was likely to be sacrificed in pursuit of breadth, thus supporting the views of many teachers in our own study.

Objective evidence for the increased workloads of infant teachers during the year following the introduction of the National Curriculum was also provided in a study of teacher time and curriculum manageability at Key Stage 1 carried out by Campbell and Neill (1992) for the Assistant Masters and Mistresses Association (now the Association of Teachers and Lecturers). This was based on written evidence from over 100 infant teachers from sixty-one LEAs in England and Wales, although the authors did not claim that this constituted a nationally representative sample. The sample was heavily biased towards 'Year 2' infant teachers (that is, of 6 to 7-year-old children) since they comprised nearly two-thirds of it.

The teachers kept a detailed record of their time spent on work for a period of seven consecutive days in 1992. The study found that, on average, the teachers worked a fifty-two hour week in 1992 (ten hours per day). This was a slight increase upon the average times recorded in previous phases of the study carried out in 1990 and 1991, and a major increase upon the average figure of forty-four hours recorded in a separate study carried out in 1971. The authors attributed the infant teachers' heavy workload partly to the demands of the National Curriculum but also to their 'personal sense of conscientiousness'.

Despite this degree of teacher commitment, Campbell and Neill concluded that as it stood, the Key Stage 1 curriculum (core and non-core) was unmanageable in terms of the times officially allocated for teaching the various subjects. This, they claimed, created an impossible dilemma for conscientious teachers and was a cause of stress and a reduced sense of achievement amongst them, although no supporting evidence for the latter assertion was provided. With further educational reforms still on-stream the authors saw no reason to predict any significant reduction in the teachers' workloads. Their report also provided evidence that the workload of Year 2 teachers was significantly heavier than that of other infant teachers, probably because of the extra demands placed on them by the administration of SATs at the end of this Key Stage.

No doubt as a direct consequence of such widespread concern amongst teachers and researchers about the manageability of the National Curriculum the National Curriculum Council (NCC), in its advice to the Secretary of State for Education, recommended that each subject order should be reduced to an 'essential core' of knowledge, skills and understanding appropriate to each Key Stage (NCC, 1993a). By contrast the Chairman of the Curriculum Council for Wales (CCW) argued against making such major changes at this relatively early stage in the implementation of the National Curriculum on the grounds of the costs, uncertainty and disruption that this would cause (Daugherty, 1992).

Assessment and Record Keeping

The second major concern of our teachers was over the heavy demands upon their time and their class management skills made by the new assessment and record keeping requirements of the National Curriculum, which were seen by some teachers as reducing the time available for actually teaching the National Curriculum. Coupled with this was the view of a majority of the teachers that the formal assessment of children's knowledge and understanding at age 7 was inappropriate. This concern was also highlighted in the other research studies of the impact of the National Curriculum and in other reports. The Leverhulme Project for example reported that concerns about national assessment were dominant amongst the sample of teachers (Bennett *et al.*, 1992), and the PACE project reported the frustration and anger expressed by many teachers over the amount of time now

Summary, Discussion and Conclusions

demanded by record keeping and assessment and their fears that these activities were beginning to take over from 'real teaching' (Osborn and Pollard, 1991).

The Leverhulme Project included a sample of teachers of 5 to 7-year-old children in order to study their views on and experiences of National Curriculum assessment and testing. A large proportion of these particular teachers felt that their time for 'normal classwork' was substantially reduced by the new assessment requirements and most teachers felt themselves to be under additional stress as a consequence. Well over half of these teachers reported having to make changes in their methods of classroom organization in order to manage these new requirements. In similar vein, the NCC advice document reported widespread concern amongst teachers that arrangements for assessment and record keeping were having an unhelpful impact on curricular decisions and were cutting disproportionately into teaching time (NCC, 1993a). Also HMI (England), in a review of the implementation of the National Curriculum in its second year (1990–91), reported that the time taken up by assessment and record keeping remained a concern for many teachers and had not so far led to a general increase in the standards of teaching and learning (DFE, 1992). The specially commissioned study of infant teachers' workloads by Campbell and Neill (1992) also highlighted the disproportionate amount of time taken up by National Curriculum testing and recording.

The Pace of Change

In our own study strong concern was expressed by the headteachers about the greatly increased work load and pressure upon their class teachers following the introduction of the National Curriculum. Some headteachers also voiced their resentment at the rapid pace at which the curriculum orders had been introduced at Key Stage 1 and, in particular at the fact that significant changes had been made in some subject orders soon after their introduction. Similarly critical views were expressed by teachers in other studies and reports. The Leverhulme Project and PACE studies reported that the teachers in their samples had reacted negatively to the compressed time scale for the introduction of the National Curriculum and the stress and higher teacher work loads resulting from it (Osborn *et al.*, 1993; Bennett *et al.*, 1992). Similarly Vulliamy and Webb (1993) reported that the primary teachers in their sample of teachers attending a global education INSET project, while generally accepting the principles and content of the National Curriculum, made explicit criticisms about the speed of its implementation and the increased volume of paper work resulting from its introduction.

Learning to Cope with the National Curriculum

The positive finding of our own study that, despite the demands and pressures exerted by the National Curriculum, many of the teachers appeared to gain in confidence in their ability to meet its requirements during the first year of its implementation finds support in the HMI review of the implementation of the National Curriculum during 1990-91 (DFE, 1992). This concluded that many primary teachers were becoming more confident about the assessment of pupils' work within the National Curriculum and that curriculum planning in Key Stages 1 and 2 continued to improve as teachers began to collaborate more and as clearer and more effective subject teaching guidelines were written. In their discussion of the survey findings from the Leverhulme Primary Project Bennett *et al.* (1992) stated that, following the implementation of the National Curriculum on a highly compressed time scale, with the accompanying stress for teachers, more certainty had appeared in the system as implementation proceeded and the process of accommodation to its requirements continued to take place. This process was reflected in the changing nature of the teachers' concerns as monitored in the study.

In the light of such findings it might be suggested that as teachers' confidence in their ability to manage the requirements of the National Curriculum grows, through improved curriculum planning and classroom organization and teaching methods, the disruptive and demoralizing effects of the over-rapid introduction of the National Curriculum will prove to have been only transitory. While in our own study the headteachers were fairly evenly split in their views concerning the impact of the National Curriculum on their schools' methods of teaching and classroom organization at the infant stage it might be predicted that, as the full range of non-core subject orders comes on-stream, with the accompanying assessment, record keeping and reporting requirements, then all schools will have to make major adaptations to their existing methods. Support for this view comes from a more recent finding of the PACE Project that the proportion of class teachers who felt that they had less freedom in their choice of teaching methods than previously increased between 1990 and 1992 (Osborn *et al.*, 1993).

The Future of Cross-curricular Teaching

The trends picked out in our research study concerning the effects of the National Curriculum upon teachers' use of the topic approach were also reported by the Curriculum Council for Wales (1992c) and by Webb (1993). The PACE project also found that teachers' ability to respond to topics introduced by children and to create teaching activities around them was being eroded (Osborn *et al.*, 1993). There is no doubt that the National Curriculum is constricting the choice of topic in thematic work but there is also evidence that much more careful thought is now being given to planning the structure and progression of this work than hitherto. The 'three wise men report' (Alexander *et al.*, 1992) contained a sharp critique of the quality of much of the cross-curricular, thematic work being carried out in primary schools and one might speculate whether this would have been the case if their report had been written a year or so later. We think not; neither do we believe that the improvement in the structure and planning of this work, which we and others have reported, are wholly due either to the report or to attacks upon 'woolly progressive education'. On the contrary we believe that it is a positive outcome of the introduction of the National Curriculum and the INSET which has been provided in its support.

There is evidence from some of the studies described earlier, including our own, that teachers are now talking of the need for discrete subject teaching to complement thematic work when it is not possible to cover all of the National Curriculum content through such an approach. This could be because they now see themselves as accountable in terms of the National Curriculum orders, whereas, in the past, they might have seen themselves as accountable to the thematic approach traditionally endorsed by many LEA primary advisory services (see Alexander, 1992). Also, as part of the improved curriculum planning, groups of teachers are meeting and working collaboratively. This has improved progression and led to a consideration of the curriculum over a Key Stage as a whole. There is a sharing of specialisms and skills that benefits both teachers and pupils. We see this as another positive outcome of the National Curriculum.

In our opinion the recent questioning of the capacity of the thematic, cross-curricular approach to teaching to carry the full burden of the National Curriculum work means a re-evaluation of the notion of 'good primary practice'. For some any decline in the amount and status of thematic work would be a negative outcome of the National Curriculum. Nevertheless, while we would deplore the loss of this approach completely we see advantages in the exploration of other ways of curriculum planning. This debate about cross-curricular vs discrete subject teaching is discussed in more detail in Chapter 9.

The Role of the Headteacher

Our findings that the headteachers reported a sharper sense of their own professional accountability arising from their schools' legal responsibility for delivering the new curriculum, coupled with a heightened awareness of their role in leading and supporting their staffs, finds endorsement in two reports produced as part of the National Curriculum consultation exercises mounted in England and Wales. In the first of these, OFSTED reported that educational leadership was considered to be central to the headteacher's role and that the demands of LMS and administration were subordinate to this task. Considerable professional overload was reported by headteachers as they managed the demands from LEAs, governors, teachers and parents (OFSTED,

Summary, Discussion and Conclusions

1993a). In a document of advice and guidance produced for primary schools in Wales, the Curriculum Council for Wales (CCW, 1992a) also draws attention to the constraints upon headteachers as they strive to discharge their role as the leading professional in the school. The document recommends that high priority should be given to providing management training for headteachers in relation to their leadership roles in the management of schools, of classroom practice and of curriculum development.

The PACE Project reported that the great majority of headteachers in the study had experienced a reduction in autonomy and felt themselves subject to more constraints and controls. This sense of loss of autonomy grew between 1990 and 1992 (Croll *et al.*, 1993). The study also found that, during this period, a minority of headteachers had moved toward a rather more directed, managerial strategy for accomplishing change, although other headteachers achieved a more collaborative, 'collegial' style.

Conclusions

Our main conclusions drawn from our own study, but supported by the literature we have reviewed in this chapter are as follows:

1. While there was a general welcome by teachers for the clear planning framework provided by the National Curriculum this was offset by their widespread concern at the over-loaded curriculum, with the sheer number of attainment targets threatening the depth and quality of the children's learning.
2. Teachers of Key Stage 1 of the National Curriculum have reported a significant increase in their workloads following the introduction of the new curriculum and a strong feeling of being under pressure to reach the many attainment targets relevant to their pupils. This pressure may be adversely affecting the teaching of slower learners and children under 5 because of a reduction in their opportunities for play based, experiential learning.
3. The assessment and record keeping requirements of the National Curriculum were a major focus of the concerns

of class teachers and headteachers alike because of the demands they made upon the time and managerial skills of class teachers at the expense of their teaching time. This deep concern was coupled with the view of the majority of teachers that the formal assessment of children's educational attainments at age 7 was educationally unsound.
4 Teachers' use of thematic/topic work changed over the period of the research. Topic work became more structured in order to take in as much National Curriculum work as possible. Topics also became more focused with a trend towards science-led topics. There was also something of a move away from cross-curricular work towards discrete subject teaching, even at Key Stage 1.

Future Developments

It is vitally important to continue the process of monitoring the impact of the National Curriculum in the years to come, in order that we may be able to assess its longer term effects. This process will be complicated by the fact that further major changes to it are already in the pipeline. Such monitoring will need to be carried out at all levels from the individual school upwards. At the national level the new agencies soon to be set up by the present government, the Schools Curriculum and Assessment Authority in England, and the Curriculum and Assessment Authority in Wales, together with OFSTED, will clearly have a major role to play in this process. At the same time there will be a continuing need for independent research studies of the kind reviewed in this chapter, at least some of which should include an element of classroom based observation, preferably involving teachers themselves as researchers.

At the time of writing, the Dearing Report (NCC, 1993b) has been published as an interim response to the Secretary of State for Education's commission to look into the scope for slimming down the National Curriculum and its associated assessment and record keeping. Amongst this report's recommendations which bear upon Key Stage 1 are the following:

Summary, Discussion and Conclusions

1 Each National Curriculum subject order should be revised to distinguish between a statutory core which must be taught, and optional studies to be carried out at the discretion of the individual teacher;
2 As a result of this restructuring teachers should be allowed a specified margin of teaching time after the requirements of the National Curriculum and Religious Education have been met. The smallest margin (10 to 15 per cent) should be specified for Key Stage 1 because of the high priority accorded to the learning of the basic skills within the core subjects.
3 Standard national assessment should be retained but with a reduction in the time it requires and equal status should be given to teacher assessment in reporting to parents and others.

It is clear that, as a result of the accumulated evidence about the unmanageability of the National Curriculum in its present form and the recommendations of the Dearing Report (although interim at this stage), the next few years will see a significant easing of the demands placed upon Key Stage 1 teachers both in teaching and assessment under the National Curriculum. However many of the major educational issues raised by our study and by other studies reviewed in this chapter will remain and will need to be resolved, especially at the school level. What is now needed is a rational debate, informed by the theoretical and research literature on the one hand and by a critical self-analysis by teachers of their professional philosophies, beliefs and classroom practices on the other (see Alexander, 1992, for a useful model designed to guide the conceptual analysis of what constitutes 'good primary practice'). These issues include the relationship and balance between the teaching of the so-called basic skills and the rest of the curriculum at Key Stage 1; the relationship between the curriculum for under-5s and the National Curriculum; the identification of and provision for slower learners under the National Curriculum; and the future of cross-curricular, thematic teaching and of discrete subject teaching at the primary school stage. These issues are explored further in Part II of this book.

Part II
Selected Issues Arising from the Study

Chapter 9

Pedagogical and Curricular Issues

Introduction

Since the introduction of the National Curriculum the debate in education has expanded to include attacks on 'primary practice' and the initial training of teachers. As the formal assessment procedures spread into the secondary sector they met strong opposition culminating in the teaching unions refusing to administer the tests and the Headteachers' Association refusing to report results. As an attempt to defuse the situation a review of the National Curriculum was announced. This review was to be led by Sir Ron Dearing and was to have a short time scale. In May 1993 Sir Ron invited those interested in education to respond to four questions. (In Wales a fifth question on the order for Welsh was included.) The questions addressed the two main criticisms of the National Curriculum: the detail within the subject areas and the complexity of the assessment procedures. There was some debate, particularly in Wales, following the lead of the Chair of CCW Richard Daugherty that a period of 'no change' during which evidence was collected for a wide ranging review was a preferable path.

> In conclusion, I would therefore ask those who, for various reasons, find current Orders unsatisfactory to have patience while, with goodwill and the professional insights gained from experience, we work towards a more satisfactory framework — a second generation of curriculum Orders... Are you, and more to the point, are primary teachers ready to contemplate another upheaval in the framework? The ultimate test for me is would pupils be best served by a further period, lasting several years, of fundamental change? Should we not, while that debate is

> in progress, concentrate all our energies on making as much of a success as we can of the current framework? (Daugherty 1992: 15)

This caution in the face of the possibly destabilizing effects of further change was reiterated by some of the associations and organizations approached specifically for a response, for example the Mathematical Association.

Duncan Graham, who had served as Chair of the NCC from 1988 to 1991, comments on the fact that the NCC was not

> permitted to undertake the broad, disinterested research which I had envisaged when appointed. Changing and updating of the curriculum needs to be on the best available evidence, commissioned from reputable bodies. (Graham, 1993: 9)

In a research project instigated by the Association of Teachers and Lecturers, Rosemary Webb (1993) found that a large majority of headteachers, class teachers and advisers were convinced that what was needed now was a period of consolidation without further changes. However this was not to be.

Pedagogical Issues

Although our research focused on Key Stage 1 it is difficult to discuss this stage in isolation. In many areas Key Stage 1 and Key Stage 2 pupils attend the same schools. In some schools they may be in the same class. The headteachers who interpret the policies are often responsible for pupils in both stages and may not distinguish between them as clearly as early years experts might. Not all headteachers will have had extensive experience of teaching at Key Stage 1. For these reasons we widen the discussion in this chapter to include the whole of the primary phase.

What to Teach or How to Teach?

Despite the rhetoric that the National Curriculum was about what to teach rather than how to teach (as illustrated in the following quotation) there were pedagogical issues that arose from it.

> The National Curriculum is not a straitjacket. It provides for greater clarity and precision about *what* should be taught while enabling schools to retain flexibility about *how* they organise their teaching. (NCC, 1989a: 1; our emphasis)

The presentation of the curriculum as discrete subject packages appeared to conflict with the thematic and cross-curricular approaches beloved of the primary practitioner and advanced by such initiatives as the Technical and Vocational Education Initiative (TVEI). Despite the fact that early supporting material such as *Policy into Practice* (DES, 1989b) and *A Framework for the Whole Curriculum in Wales* (CCW, 1989) emphasized such approaches and cross-curricular themes, dimensions and competences (skills in England) were a much heralded element of the National Curriculum, they were never really treated as seriously as the individual subjects in many quarters. For example when the Council for the Accreditation of Teacher Education (CATE) queried the suitability of undergraduate degrees of students on an initial teacher training (ITT) course they indicated that relevance to the primary school curriculum did not necessarily include subjects such as economics despite the inclusion of economic awareness as a cross-curriculum theme (personal communication from CATE to Susan Sanders, 1991)

Several initiatives were run to develop materials for the teaching of such themes and dimensions but by 1993 they received only four pages of mention in CCW (1993) compared with twenty-three pages on individual subjects and appear under the heading 'other opportunities'. However Rosemary Webb reports that

> Most of the LEAs regarded the cross-curricular themes (economic and industrial understanding, careers education and guidance, health education, education for citizenship and environmental education) as important. (Webb, 1993: 75)

Teaching Methods

Robin Alexander's report on the Primary Needs Initiative in Leeds (Alexander, 1991) followed by the government-commissioned report by Alexander, Rose and Woodhead (1992) were instrumental in raising the debate about the efficacy of 'good primary practice'. Good primary practice is something that is rarely defined but has a meaning for practitioners.[1]

It is perhaps because of this lack of explicit definition that it has proved easy to attack it and to undermine teachers' confidence in it. This debate about primary practice, tied with the notion that the National Curriculum and its associated formal assessment procedure would raise standards within schools, led to re-examination of the way that younger school pupils are taught. Out of this came calls for 'subject specialist' teaching and this was backed up by the new proposals for the initial training of teachers (DFE, 1993). As these proposals also included provision for non-graduate teachers of nursery and Key Stage 1 pupils it could have been possible for the curriculum implications to have been lost.[2]

A simple way to change practice within the primary school is to prepare teachers to teach only in a certain way. The pedagogy of institutions had been under concerted attack with limited success. By legislating for a narrower curriculum and more time spent on the basic elements of the core subjects the government might expect to end up with a teaching force with a totally different notion of 'good primary practice'.

In this chapter we suggest ways that the manner in which the National Curriculum is taught is being influenced and manipulated. We highlight implications of both a curricular and pedagogical nature for educationalists and teachers of Key Stage 1 pupils in particular.

Single Subjects or Whole Curriculum?

In 1989 the Early Years Curriculum Group wrote

> The documents published by the National Curriculum Council are very encouraging in the way in which they

explicitly endorse good primary practice. A number of ideas which permeate these documents assert and affirm the very principles on which the early years curriculum is founded. (Early Years Curriculum Group, 1989: 21)

The group's writing indicates a wholesale commitment to a cross-curricular approach.

However we have argued in Chapter 4 that this belief may be at best dated and at worst naive. The interest in Robin Alexander's work in particular, from the report into primary education in Leeds in 1991 which led to the report on curriculum organization and classroom practice in primary schools by Alexander, Rose and Woodhead (the 'three wise men'), focused media attention on the obvious shortcomings of some thematic, topic and cross-curricular approaches. Unfortunately the media attention was not balanced and in many instances the positive findings were ignored.

The report described topic work as 'very undemanding' with negligible opportunities for progression. The quality of planning was questioned. Monitoring and assessment of topic work were described as weak.

As an alternative way of meeting such criticisms we were offered the notion of subject specialist teaching in the primary school: 'Subject teaching has an essential place in modern primary education' (Alexander *et al.*, 1992: 35, para. 123). However the paragraph goes on to say

When topic work focuses on a clearly defined and limited number of attainment targets it, too, can make an important contribution to the development of pupil learning.

Our research indicates that this is the new style of topic work, highly focused and carefully planned with attainment targets in mind.

Duncan Graham (1993) is more sceptical in his evaluation of the three wise men's suggestions for subject specialism.

How much of the talk of specialism was politically inspired and was it educationally sound? The arguments must be as strong for extending primary methods upwards into secondary schools — as so many successful middle-schools do — as for the introduction of earlier specialisation. (Graham 1993: 123)

Whether politically inspired or not there is certainly evidence that groups have begun to explore other ways of 'delivering the curriculum'.

Webb (1993: 69) reports

In one authority the message on the courses over the past year, which was initially disseminated at a headteachers' conference, has been that 'the global topic planned through flow diagrams is outdated and doesn't take account of the structure of the National Curriculum'.

As primary teachers struggle to cover the breadth of the National Curriculum they try various strategies.

Tyler (1992) discusses what he sees as the 'bipolar construct "cross-curricular" versus "single subject" '. He reports two views coming across from primary teachers. On the one hand there is a group of teachers who feel that the only way to manage the 334 statements of attainment so far detailed is by a cross-curricular approach. On the other hand there is another group of teachers who argue for a 'more discrete approach to the primary curriculum'. It is because of the complex nature of the documents that they see the task of meshing them together as too great. They take the fact that the documents are single subject in nature that the curriculum should be taught in the same way. We too heard these two views expressed by teachers (see Chapter 4).

For Tyler (1993) the two views come from different teachers, but how many teachers struggle to reconcile what they perceive to be pedagogically sound but unmanageable as against a style with which they have little faith pedagogically but makes the everyday running of their teaching so much easier to manage? The conflicting messages over time from the NCC, the CCW, etc. only serve to confuse.

Tyler (1993: 4) identifies three main curricular styles in current use.

These three styles can be characterised by the differing degrees of integration and differentiation in the curriculum; they are approaches which emphasise (i) individual subjects, (ii) subject specific topics or (iii) thematic planning.

Graham (1993: 119) does not see the pressures to change teaching methods as coming from the nature of the National Curriculum but from

> a tide of romantic traditionalism, a gut response to ministers' own school-days, and an over reaction to anecdotal evidence of the perceived dangers of extreme teaching methods.

Whatever the government's reasons for pushing for change in teaching methods (and we do not necessarily disagree with Graham's interpretation) they have cleverly chosen not to legislate the methods of teaching but to subtly influence them.

Changing Pedagogy

The Collins English Dictionary defines pedagogy as 'the principles, practice or profession of teaching'. All of these have been subject to pressure to change since the introduction of the National Curriculum. In the next part of this chapter we focus on several ways in which this pressure has been exerted.

The Role of Curriculum Guidance (NCC, CCW and the LEAs) as Change Agent

Tyler (1992) reports that some of the guidelines suggest the use of curriculum specialists. He comments as we do in Chapter 4 that initially and now superficially the non-statutory guidelines support a cross-curricular approach. This support can be seen as strong and directive initially but now superficial and soft. Topic work had a similar fate (see Chapter 4).

Pedagogical and Curricular Issues

We argued in Chapter 4 that this support changes over time so that by the time of writing (summer 1993) the support is minimal from both NCC and CCW. In fact we interpret this as these bodies 'selling out' the primary practitioners who followed their earlier directives, for the sake of the rhetoric of the New Right. Rosemary Webb (1993) highlights one LEA's strong antithematic approach for Key Stage 2 (see above).

To what extent can teachers at Key Stage 1 hold on to the thematic approach? The formal testing procedures crumbled not because of the sensible and measured reactions of the Key Stage 1 teachers who had tried them out but because of the strongly unionized Key Stage 3 teachers' response *before* they had tried them out. How empowered do Key Stage 1 teachers feel to withstand the explicit and implicit pressures to move away from thematic, cross-curricular approaches and towards single subject teaching?

As the support for thematic, topic and cross-curricular approaches from the likes of NCC, CCW and LEAs diminishes how can the demoralization of teachers be stemmed? So far the arguments for the maintenance of such approaches have been based on dogma: for instance the romantic image of young children and teachers tripping through the wet grass was used by Gammage during a lecture defending 'good primary practice' at University College, Swansea in 1992. (Gammage, 1992) What is needed is extensive and rigorous research into the benefits of such approaches. The evidence has to be of a quality to dispel the hysteria of the New Right. Teacher organizations and individual teachers can support and participate in such research.

The Role of Assessment as Change Agent

The government knew that it is often the assessment procedures that drive the teaching approach. Despite the rhetoric of the guidelines and the 'hands off' approach of the orders in terms of teaching styles influence is exerted through the formalized assessment procedures. Kelly (1990) in his discussion of the assessment and testing programme within the National Curriculum refers to the 'backlash effects' that testing has on the curriculum.

Caroline Gipps, writing in 1988, had no doubts that 'on the

basis of what we know already about the effects of testing' that regular and significant testing would affect several elements of primary school practice. These included

- a variety of teaching and learning approaches,
- the integration of some subjects into topic work,
- [few] lessons in formal subjects, other than maths [sic].
 (Gipps, 1988: 71)

The change in the approach to teaching of mathematics (away from the purely didactic; including investigative and problem-solving approaches) is attributed by many not to the Cockcroft Report or to the work of the advisory teachers but to the inclusion of a coursework element in GCSE.[3]

The impact of testing on teaching was recognized in 1988 by the National Society for the Study of Education in the USA.

> In recent years, it seems that the aims of education, the business of our schools, and the goals of educational reform are addressed not so much in terms of curriculum — the courses of study that are followed — as they are in terms of standardized tests. It is testing, not the 'official' stated curriculum, that is increasingly determining what is taught, how it is taught, what is learned, and how it is learned. (Madeus, 1988: 83)

The testing procedures for Key Stage 1 (and for Key Stage 2) are *not* cross-curricular in nature. Individual subjects are tested separately. What message does this send to teachers?

Nigel Proctor warned in 1990 that the focus on subject testing suggested to him that cross-curricular issues could face extinction. To what extent will his prediction prove correct? Will Key Stage 1 become a conservation area for such issues until former primary practice grows strong and flourishes in captivity, able to defend itself against the criticisms of Alexander *et al.* (1992) and others and thence to re-populate Key Stage 2 and beyond? Or will Key Stage 1 become the Galápagos or Madame Tussauds' of the thematic approach, visited with nostalgia by past practitioners and young teachers but, like steam railways, an enjoyable pastime with little relevance in the real world of the big school? The choice is ours, not just that of the teachers of Key Stage 1 pupils.

Topic work can certainly be like Alexander *et al.*'s (1992) worst scenario. However they were criticizing the current implementation of the approach, not the approach itself. Unfortunately much of the defence was erroneously centred on the sentiment 'Oh no it isn't like that', which was not strictly true, rather than a focus on putting it right. Defendants appeared to be defending the indefensible — poor classroom practice. They did the approach no service.

The National Curriculum has allowed the professionals to do what Alexander *et al.* suggested it could, namely improve the delivery without rejecting the approach. NCC and CCW should recognize this fact and make explicit their support for the approach when it is used well. This would increase Key Stage 1 teachers' confidence in their use of this approach and would legitimize it.

Teachers need to be confident in their commitment to thematic, topic and cross-curricular approaches. Tyler (1992: 8) concludes that

> Despite the current modifications to the assessment programme at Key Stages 1 and 2, the main emphasis in testing will continue to be on individual subjects within the curriculum. The danger is that the current cross-curricular and thematic approaches which are used so effectively in many schools will be replaced by a highly differentiated, and possibly fragmented, curriculum.

In August 1993 Sir Ron Dearing published the results of his review of the National Curriculum. At Key Stage 1 only English and mathematics are to be assessed by external tests. Science is to be tested only by statutory teacher assessment. The elements of English and mathematics to be tested are much reduced (NCC, 1993b). The possible impact of this on the curriculum is discussed in the second part of this chapter.

The Impact of National Curriculum

Initial Teacher Training as an Agent of Change

Another way in which the government has sought to influence the teaching of the curriculum has been through the regulations governing the training of teachers. If teachers are trained to teach a certain content in a certain way, then they may well hold on to that, whatever the accepted craft knowledge in the schools in which they teach. By regulating the training that teachers receive, a government may well expect eventually to change the practice within schools.

From 1989 onwards the CATE regulations stipulated the number of hours that students should study and be taught English (and Welsh in Welsh-medium schools), mathematics and science — the core subjects of the National Curriculum. This limited the number of hours available for the rest of the primary school curriculum and led to debates, particularly within the PGCE programme, as to the feasibility of training students to teach all the subjects within the time span of the existing training programme. This coupled with the attack on the philosophy and experience of teacher trainers leading to calls for more school based work (and the resulting depletion in available hours in college) is reflected in the new proposals (Welsh Office, 1993; DFE, 1993).

There is an emphasis in the HMI report (OFSTED, 1993b: 2) on the time problem within ITT courses.

> Poor quality provision often resulted from inadequate time allocation rather than poor preparation or delivery. The content of a few courses did not fully cover the National Curriculum content required in primary schools.

The new proposals for the training of primary school teachers (DFE, 1993) introduce the notion of subject specialist teachers and teachers not being trained to teach all the subjects in the curriculum. However with the latter there are conflicting messages, particularly as the proposals refer on occasions to the National Curriculum (for example DFE, 1993: 7, para. 11) and on other occasions to the primary curriculum (for example DFE, 1993: 7, para. 12). Indeed in paragraph 21 both are used without any definition or distinction being made.

> ... wishes to encourage the use of specialist teaching in primary schools, particularly at Key Stage 2[4] (Welsh Office, 1993: para. 13)

> Newly qualified teachers should be able to demonstrate relevant knowledge and understanding of the National Curriculum, including testing and assessment arrangements, in the core subjects and those other foundation subjects *covered by their course.* (Welsh Office, 1993: Annex A, para. 2.3) (our italics)

> The new criteria do not therefore require all courses to cover all subjects of the primary curriculum ... (Welsh Office, 1993: para.15)

However some clarification is offered:

> It is expected that, for the time being, most courses will continue to prepare students to teach the full primary curriculum. (Welsh Office, 1993: para. 14)

The statements of competences included in the 1993 proposals for initial teacher training require the new teachers to demonstrate relevant knowledge and understanding of the National Curriculum. As the National Union of Teachers (1993) response to those proposals pointed out there was no reference to the need for new teachers to demonstrate knowledge of the *whole* curriculum. Alexander *et al.* (1992: 35, para. 121) commented

> The subject knowledge required by the National Curriculum makes it unlikely that the generalist primary teacher will be able to teach all subjects in the depth required. This is particularly the case in Key Stage 2, but is true also in Key Stage 1.

The new proposals emphasize the fragmented curriculum rather than the curriculum as an entity. Will this lead to a generation of teachers who see the curriculum not as a coherent whole but as made up of discrete packets of subjects that do not support, overlap or interact with each other? Is there an over-emphasis on subject as curriculum orders? Course evaluations from last year's primary phase PGCE students at the authors' institution included requests for more emphasis on the National Curriculum document in mathematics. One author's efforts to teach the students about mathematics as a *context* for the orders had not worked. They saw mathematics as the orders.

Students quite rightly perceive practising teachers as experts in the delivery of the National Curriculum. Teachers working with students can help. They can 'hold the dream' of good primary practice, and help students to work in a variety of ways by interpreting the National Curriculum Orders while maintaining their integrity. We should not forget the rhetoric from NCC quoted on page 134 that the National Curriculum is about what to teach rather than how to teach it.

The initial teacher training (primary) proposals also allow for the development of new courses; 'However, more courses may be developed to cover parts of the primary curriculum in greater depth' (Department for Education, 1993: para. 14). Such courses will have to be developed by higher education institutions in partnership with schools. If neither are willing is the government prepared to instruct or influence with funding? We note a lack of success with such tactics in recent months. Secondary schools were instructed to carry out Key Stage 3 testing; most did not. Opting out was accompanied by financial benefits; to date many schools have rejected opting out of LEA control.

Curricular Issues

The Effect on the Curriculum

To some extent it is inappropriate to separate pedagogical and curriculum issues and in the preceding part of this chapter we have dealt with some curriculum aspects. However there is a fundamental issue which we have left to deal with separately and this is the way in which aspects of the National Curriculum change our overall view of what the curriculum, the primary school curriculum and the early years curriculum, might be.

Pedagogical and Curricular Issues

Let us imagine for the moment a national curriculum which accounts for 100 per cent of the content. The subjects of this national curriculum are art, drama, music and dance for the first three years, then the humanities are included and finally when pupils reach the age of 11 mathematics, science and language and literature are taught as well. What does this tell us about the society? Which subjects does that society perceive as the most important? Which subjects would parents ask about on open evenings? What skills are employers looking for?

Now let us imagine that the government of that country wants, for whatever reason, to embrace a broader curriculum but not to lose sight of the traditional values of the society. Why not insist that all the subjects are taught from the beginning of formal education but only test art, drama, music and dance at the end of the first three years and so on? Would that not serve your purpose? If a subject is tested it must be important!

Now to return to our own National Curriculum. Never mind the rhetoric; what will the effect of the new testing procedures be on the early years' curriculum? What distortions will appear? Will teachers continue to struggle with technology or Welsh if the pupils are not to be formally tested in those subjects (see Chapter 11)?

Our teachers told us in 1993 that subjects that have to be formally tested have a heightened focus and that 'teaching to the tests' is already happening. The curriculum is already changing under the pressure of the formal assessment procedures. How will history view the outcomes of revisions driven by the teachers' concerns?

If the amount of time that has to be spent on the orders is cut down, as Dearing (NCC, 1993b) proposes, will teachers use the saved time for thematic work, for example, or will they fill all the available time with the National Curriculum? What are the tensions between Key Stage 1 and Key Stage 2? Do they still have distinctive elements? Should the approach to teaching be different in each Key Stage? Should there be a different, more limited curriculum for Key Stage 1 with greater emphasis upon learning the basic skills (see Chapters 10 and 11, and Dearing, 1993)?

Do teachers have a view of assessment as distinct from

teaching? Do they need to remind themselves that assessment is part of teaching? Certainly some of the teachers in our study seemed to have (see Chapters 3 and 4) but they may have been referring to the summative kinds of assessment rather than the formative when they made statements contrasting testing with teaching. Would this remove some of their concerns? Teachers found the management of the earlier pedagogically sound assessment procedures difficult. They may have found themselves accepting tests that were easier to manage but pedagogically unsound. Dearing helps as he raises the status of teacher assessment and acknowledges some of the failings of standardized assessment tasks.

Conclusions

During the course of our study there was a change from the almost automatic acceptance by teachers of the thematic approach as *the* approach during the primary years. Different approaches such as focused topic work, discrete subject teaching and teaching by subject specialists are being explored. The wider debate about the breadth of curriculum available at Key Stage 1 may just be beginning. An explicit debate is to be welcomed; manipulation of the curriculum by other means is not.

Notes

1 For an extensive discussion readers could refer to Chapter 11 in Alexander, 1992.
2 This is particularly possible as much of the discontent at the proposals focused on this element with the teacher unions also questioning the partnership proposals between schools and higher education institutions.
3 We have heard this sentiment attributed to Professor Hugh Burkhardt several times but have never seen it written. Broadfoot *et al.* (1991b: 153) quote 'What you test is what you get' and attribute it to Burkhardt (1989). However no publication details are provided in the references and this particular reference could not be traced despite personal correspondence with the authors.
4 This encouragement is not exclusively at Key Stage 2, however!

Chapter 10

Slower Learners and Socially Disadvantaged Children

In our study well over half of the class teachers, both in 1989 and 1990, judged that they had some pupils in their classes with special educational needs, even though only a handful of Key Stage 1 children in the sample schools had been formally statemented (see Chapter 2). The reported learning difficulties of these children were particularly related to speech, language and reading and some children were described as showing behaviour difficulties which affected their concentration and sometimes caused disruption in class. In terms of the Warnock Report (DES, 1978) and the 1981 Education Act, the majority of these 'slower learners' would probably be described as having mild or moderate learning difficulties, with a smaller number perhaps showing specific learning difficulties in language, reading or number. Some of them would, in addition, show emotional or behavioural difficulties. In some cases these children's learning problems may have been caused, at least in part, by factors such as specific learning difficulties, physical or sensory difficulties or limited general ability (DES, 1978).

However, given that one-third of the sample schools served predominantly working-class or lower working-class areas (including five schools formerly designated as social priority area (SPA) schools), it is also very likely that many of the children would have come from socially disadvantaged home backgrounds. Such homes, for reasons of poverty, family disruption or lack of parental awareness, do not provide the parental and family support for their learning which is such a crucial component in children's early education, with the result that these children enter school with a low level of pre-literacy and other skills and knowledge upon which infant school teachers can build. Starting

The Impact of the National Curriculum

from a lower educational base than children from more favoured backgrounds, these children are more likely to make comparatively slower progress in learning the basic skills, and the 'achievement gap' between them and the former may widen progressively during their primary and secondary school years (Cox, 1982). While it is very important not to equate working-class membership with social disadvantage, the majority of disadvantaged children tend to come from families characterized by lower occupational status or long term unemployment (Davie *et al.*, 1972; Wedge and Essen, 1982).

Effects of the National Curriculum on Slower Learners

Access to the National Curriculum

Both the class teachers and the headteachers were asked how they thought the introduction of the National Curriculum was affecting the slower learning children. Their responses were summarized in Chapter 5. While a proportion of the teachers claimed that these children were largely unaffected by the introduction of the National Curriculum and continued to work at their own pace and level as before, many more expressed serious concern about its impact upon their learning. In particular they were worried that pressure was being placed upon them to achieve the relevant attainment targets at the same time as their classmates and that this pressure undermined the quality of their learning with respect to understanding and level of skill mastery. Further, the requirement that these children should be taught the full range of National Curriculum subjects, including Welsh as a second language since the schools were located in Wales, meant that there was insufficient time to teach them the basic skills of reading, writing, spelling and number to an adequate level of mastery. As reported in Chapter 6, both of these concerns were expressed by some teachers with regard to Year 1 children in general but, presumably, the level of concern was greater with regard to slower learning children.

At least some of the teachers voicing such concerns were

anxious that their slower learning pupils should not be disadvantaged in relation to their classroom peers when it came to formal assessment (through SATs) of their attainments at age 7. They felt that if these children performed relatively poorly in the tests, their 'failure' would be public and consequently more damaging to their self-esteem. These teachers appeared to be caught in the dilemma that pushing the slower learners too hard would impair the quality of their learning, particularly of the basic skills, but not pushing them hard enough would lead to their subsequent low achievement in formal assessment and damaged self-esteem.

Such concerns regarding the prospects for the slower learning children find support in a document produced by the NCC (1993c) on the topic of special needs and the National Curriculum which was based on the views of teachers in special schools, special units in ordinary schools and in special support services. The document distinguishes between 'exceptionally severe' (profound and multiple) learning difficulties and 'other' learning difficulties of the kind described earlier in this chapter. While strongly endorsing the principle of the entitlement of all pupils to a broad, balanced and relevant curriculum, including the National Curriculum, the teachers identified several issues of concern regarding the teaching of slower learning children, including the following:

1 The links between the Key Stages and chronological ages are reported to be unrealistic for this group of pupils. Many need to work at National Curriculum levels below those designated for the Key Stage, whilst still having access to age-appropriate programmes of study;
2 Although these pupils may progress more slowly than their peers, they could still gain full access to the National Curriculum programmes of study at a later date;
3 Other priorities, such as speech therapy, extra time on reading and mathematics and life skills, mean that the time available for National Curriculum subjects is reduced;
4 Teachers suggest that there should be non-mandatory Standard Assessment Tasks for this group of pupils and much greater emphasis on teacher assessment. (NCC, 1993c: 5)

Clearly, like some of the teachers in our study, these teachers appear to be seeking official acknowledgment of the slower pace of learning of pupils with a variety of learning difficulties that are not accompanied by a formal statement of special educational need under the 1981 Education Act, and more flexibility in the framework of the National Curriculum to accommodate their needs. Under present regulations the processes available to schools for adapting the requirements of the National Curriculum to meet individual learning needs involve making formal statements of special educational needs or formal exemptions (disapplications) or modifications to it. All of these are somewhat bureaucratic processes and, as Lewis (1991) points out, the heavy statutory emphasis upon these procedures sits uneasily with the rhetoric of the National Curriculum which stresses its suitability for all children. Lewis argues that if the National Curriculum is really attuned to individual learning needs then there should be no need for formal disapplications or modifications. It should be stressed, however, that in an earlier publication focusing upon children with special educational needs, the National Curriculum Council envisaged that only a few pupils should require exceptional arrangements for modifications or exemptions and only when the NC requirements prove impossible to achieve or are inappropriate to the pupil's very specialized needs (NCC, 1989b). In its later (1993c) publication it reports teachers' rejection of the 'negative concept of disapplication' and their request for a more positive approach to access to the National Curriculum for pupils with special educational needs.

Pending some rewriting of the National Curriculum orders and regulations to provide the necessary flexibility in responding to the wide variety of children's individual learning needs, teachers will have to continue to work under the present legislative framework but they will need advice and support in resolving the dilemma outlined above. Perhaps their concerns about the public 'failure' of slower learning children to achieve the same attainment target levels as their classmates at the end of Key Stage 1 would be eased by their own acceptance of the fact that the range of variation in children's learning needs and capabilities will be reflected in different levels of attainment when these are formally assessed. This acknowledgment would by no means justify teachers holding low expectations of their slower learning pupils' potential levels of attainment but it would perhaps help them to avoid over-pressurizing these children.

Learning Basic Skills

It is a fundamental aim of primary (infant) education to secure in all children the foundations of the skills of language, literacy and numeracy, upon which so much of the learning in other curriculum areas is built. To achieve this aim, infant teachers need to allocate sufficient time in the curriculum to provide the necessary learning experiences, both informally at the level of pre-literacy and pre-numeracy skills and awareness, and in a more direct and structured fashion in the later stages. Our study findings have raised the question of whether the wider subject requirements of the National Curriculum have unduly constrained the time available for the teaching of the basic skills, particularly for slower learning children.

On this question reports from government-appointed agencies seem somewhat conflicting. In its recent advice to the Secretary of State for Education the NCC (1993a, para. 2.3) expressed the particular concern of teachers that the breadth of the National Curriculum meant that 'there is now insufficient time to teach the basics of reading, writing, spelling and arithmetic which are essential to all future learning'. Such concern was probably one of the factors which led this body to recommend that the various subject orders of the National Curriculum should be slimmed down to an 'essential core' of knowledge, understanding and skills appropriate to each Key Stage. Similar concern was voiced by infant teachers throughout Wales as reported in a document produced by the CCW compiled in the process of carrying out consultations with schools, teachers and LEAs concerning the National Curriculum (CCW, 1992c). In contrast OFSTED, in its report in 1993, based upon HMI school inspections and consultations with teachers and schools, made the following observation: 'Although there was some concern that as a result of introducing the National Curriculum, the time for teaching the basic skills of literacy, and to a lesser extent numeracy, was being "squeezed", most teachers in Key Stages 1 and 2 *devoted at least sufficient time to these aspects of the work.*' (OFSTED, 1993: 7. Our italics). However this report also commented that intakes of pupils varied markedly in respect of readiness for school work, making it necessary for some schools, mainly those serving disadvantaged areas, to give more attention and time to teaching reading than elsewhere.

In a specially commisioned study Campbell and Neill (1992) analysed the working week of a sample of infant teachers. They found that, far from there being a shortage of time for English and mathematics, the large amount of teaching time devoted to the core subjects, and to English in particular, did not leave enough time for teaching the non-core subjects and religious education. In one of their analyses 56 per cent of the teacher's week, on average, was spent on core subjects, 30 per cent on non-core subjects and 12 per cent on teacher assessment and SAT administration. In their view the teachers' emphasis on core subject teaching was squeezing out reasonable time for other subjects and thus making it impossible to deliver a balanced and broadly based curriculum as required by the 1988 Education Reform Act.

At the time of writing, the Secretary of State for Education has announced plans for a slimming down both of the subject orders and of the associated testing procedures. This should certainly help teachers in their task of balancing the need to spend sufficient time in teaching the basic skills to slower learning and other pupils with that of simultaneously covering the whole curriculum. Even so schools serving socially disadvantaged areas will still need to devote relatively more time to teaching reading and other basic skills than other schools, as the OFSTED (1993a) report made clear. However, as perhaps was hinted in that report, there is a danger that teachers can spend *too much* time on teaching the basic skills to slower learning and socially disadvantaged children, with the result that these children may not experience the full range of the wider curriculum which is their entitlement. In our own study, although few teachers reported benefits from the National Curriculum for slower learning children, some of those who did so mentioned that these children were experiencing a richer curriculum than before, which now included science and technology.

As Lewis (1991) points out, curricula for children with learning difficulties in both mainstream and special schools have in the past been criticized as being too restricted and concentrated on the narrow teaching of the basic skills. In his analytical study of the work of the schools participating in the Leeds Primary Needs Project, many of which served socially disadvantaged areas, Alexander (1992) concluded that too much time was allocated to language and maths, given that the children were observed to be spending less of their time working and more time being distracted in these subjects than in others. This may have been partly due to the formal nature of the basic skills work being required of them which emphasized reading and writing at the expense of listening and speaking. Despite the the greater allocation of time and resources to the teaching of the basic skills in these project schools there was no evidence of a subsequent rise in the children's measured reading standards.

Another negative consequence of an over-concentration of curriculum time on the teaching of basic skills is that valuable opportunities for the children's developing writing and reading skills to be reinforced in the context of other curriculum learning, such as in science or history, are reduced.

The planned reduction of the National Curriculum load should benefit all children, but particularly slower learners for whom the pressures to progress on all fronts, described by our teachers, should be eased. However the reduction of curriculum overload and the allocation of sufficient, but not too much time to the teaching of the basic skills will not in themselves be enough to ensure the successful learning and progress of these children.

Assessment and Recording

What is also needed is a skilful and sensitive exploration of each child's learning difficulties and strengths in a given curriculum area and a careful matching of the learning tasks chosen to each child's profile of skills and understanding at any given stage. In addition the teacher must also select teaching methods that are appropriate both to the task and to the child's learning needs. All this represents a challenge to the class teacher's professional skills and curricular knowledge. In its report on the implementation of the National Curriculum during its second year, for example, HMI found that the principal difficulty facing teachers at all Key Stages and in all subjects was the matching of learning tasks to the abilities of individual pupils (DFE, 1992), although they comment that teachers were becoming more aware than before of the precise level of pupils' achievements and needs through improved curriculum planning and assessment. In the NCC document on special needs and the National Curriculum referred to earlier (NCC, 1993c), the teachers consulted identified a need for guidance on differentiating teaching across all ability ranges but particularly for pupils with special educational needs and the exceptionally able.

As Alexander (1992) points out, a satisfactory matching of curriculum task to individual learning needs requires, amongst other things, that the teacher has an adequate depth of curriculum knowledge in the given subject to be able to diagnose each child's learning needs. While this requirement applies equally strongly to both core and non-core subjects it seems to be in the latter that primary teachers feel most insecure in this respect (Bennett *et al.*, 1992). Nevertheless, for all subjects, including those concerned with the teaching of the basic skills, an adequate level of INSET provision and back-up classroom advisory support for the teacher is essential if the challenge of meeting children's individual learning needs within the framework of the National Curriculum is to be met. In this connection it is disturbing to note HMI's comment that the reduction in the number of advisory teachers and the need for the latter to concentrate on other issues, in consequence of other changes stemming from the ERA, has deprived schools of valuable support (DFE, 1992).

While it cannot make up for a shortfall in good INSET provision and back-up advisory support, the class teacher can find some helpful guidance in publications dealing with the teaching of children with special needs within the framework of the National Curriculum, such as the NCC's (1989b) document entitled *A Curriculum for All*. This states that, in the process of giving pupils with special educational needs the opportunity to demonstrate their performance levels on the statements of attainment, teachers will often find it necessary to structure their schemes of work in such a way as to provide a series of intermediate goals. They will also need to adapt their record systems to reflect these small steps towards the statements of attainment. This approach of breaking down teaching sequences into smaller than usual steps to meet the needs of slower learning children is generally known as curriculum based teaching, or sometimes objectives based teaching, and it has many advocates (for example Solity and Bull, 1987). However, as the NCC's (1989b) document points out, some attainment targets are more difficult to break down into smaller steps than others. Moreover, Lewis (1991) argues that in planning teaching activities designed to help children with learning difficulties to reach particular statements of attainment, it is more profitable to focus on the relevant programmes of study, rather than simply to break down the former.

The book by Lewis is a valuable source of practical guidance to the teacher on teaching children with special needs. Another useful source is the book by Chazan *et al.* (1991) on helping 5 to 8-year-olds with special educational needs. This includes a good discussion of the construction of individual learning programmes for children and is illustrated with case studies.

In addition to the diagnostic assessment of children's strengths and weaknesses in a particular aspect of learning which was discussed earlier, teachers will need to carry out regular assessment and recording of their children's progress towards the various core curriculum statements of attainment. Given that the three levels of performance reflected by these statements at Key Stage 1 are relatively crude, it is important for the teacher to devise a finer graded system for recording the progress of slower learning pupils. Otherwise there is a real danger that the more subtle, but nevertheless real progress made by such children towards a particular statement of attainment will go unrecorded, which could be demotivating for the teacher as well as the pupil. Checklists can be useful in this respect but some of these have been criticized as superficial by HMI (DES, 1990a). The curriculum or objectives based methods of teaching referred to earlier have their own built-in assessment and recording systems which can be readily adapted to the National Curriculum. Also Lewis (1991) provides helpful suggestions concerning the use of classroom observation by the teacher in identifying children's individual learning needs, and the use of individual records as a means of recording the progress of slower learning pupils towards particular learning objectives within the National Curriculum.

The Role of the Teacher

The problems discussed so far in this chapter have largely focused on the effects of the National Curriculum upon slower learning children. Equally important is the impact of the National Curriculum upon the teachers since their morale, attitudes and professional skills are the crucial determinant of the children's academic progress. There was evidence from our own study of a concern by teachers in schools serving predominantly socially disadvantaged areas that their professional skills were being called into question in the light of the new climate of the schools' public accountability for their pupils' academic achievement and progress. As one teacher put it,

> Teachers are under pressure to analyse what children are learning and when they review it and the children do not make progress it is demoralizing for the staff.

Another teacher referred to the 'immense pressure on the class teacher to get poorly motivated children to a reasonable standard' and expressed the concern that poor work by the children would be interpreted as poor teaching. The headteacher of a socially disadvantaged area school expressed his concern that in view of the low level of attainment by most pupils in the school and the lack of parental support, the publication of formal test results (SATs) would in no way reflect the hard work and dedication of the staff. Taking this point further, another headteacher working in a similar school pointed out that in order to interpret the Key Stage 1 test results fairly it is necessary to know the children's starting levels on school entry so that the children's progress can be evaluated. Ironically, given the current strong backlash amongst both teachers and parents against all formal

National Curriculum testing, this would argue for the creation of some form of testing of school entry skills at age 5.

The relatively low academic attainments of socially disadvantaged children have been well documented in Britain (Davie et al., 1972; Cox and Jones, 1983) and one cannot deny that schools serving predominantly disadvantaged areas face a formidable challenge to their professional skills in ensuring that their pupils reach acceptable levels of academic achievement across the full range of the National Curriculum subjects. A particular burden falls upon infant teachers in such schools since they are teaching children whose entry skills in many cases are relatively low and their task is to lay the foundations of oracy, literacy and numeracy upon which the children's future school progress depends. However it is vital that, in trying to meet this challenge, teachers should maintain positive attitudes and expectations towards their socially disadvantaged pupils and not prejudge their capabilities. Indeed the so called 'three wise men' report (Alexander et al., 1992) stresses the importance of all schools having the highest expectations of their pupils and claims that standards in primary schools will not rise until teachers expect more of their pupils, in particular the more able and the disadvantaged children.

There is a good deal of evidence that many teachers underestimate the capabilities of their socially disadvantaged pupils, for example from the study of the progress of children attending infant schools in the inner London area (Tizard et al., 1988) and in the study of Leeds primary schools by Alexander (1992) already referred to. Alexander concluded that the way in which the Leeds Primary Needs Project was being implemented encouraged a deficit view of disadvantaged children which concentrated on what they could not do rather than on what they were capable of. In their joint discussion paper Alexander et al. (1992) claim that in some schools there has been a tendency to stereotype children and assume that social disadvantage inevitably leads to educational failure. It may be that some of the teachers in our own study were falling into this trap. Further evidence came in OFSTED's (1993a) report on curriculum organization and practice in primary schools. This states that amongst the issues raised in the follow-up conferences,

> there was surprisingly little sense of the urgency to need to know in some detail the existing standards of pupils' performance in literacy and numeracy and the direction in which standards were moving. Nor was there sufficient appreciation of how assessment information could be used to plan programmes of work for individuals, groups or classes. (OFSTED 1993: para. 28)

If one accepts such evidence for the widespread under-expectation by many teachers of the capabilities of their socially disadvantaged and slower learning pupils, the urgent question arises as to what can be done to eradicate it. Part of the solution, as has already been discussed, lies in enhancing teachers' diagnostic skills and curricular knowledge so that they match learning tasks more closely to individual children's needs without prejudging their future capabilities. For Alexander (1992) this is the key requirement in the raising of teachers' expectations. Other pointers come from the study carried out by Mortimore *et al.* (1988) into the differential effectiveness of a sample of inner London primary/junior schools in raising their pupils' educational attainments. This study found that, while the social class grouping of the parents was the most powerful determinant of the children's initial attainments at age 7, their subsequent progress up to age 11 was more closely related to the quality of the education they received in their primary/junior schools. Despite the fact that they served similar catchment areas, some schools were more effective than others in boosting the educational performance of their socially disadvantaged pupils as well as that of children from more advantaged home backgrounds. The authors stress that while the more successful schools were characterized by their smaller size, good physical environment, stability of teaching staff and covered the full primary age range, as well as having voluntary status, these were not the crucial factors accounting for their better overall performance. The most important factors accounting for the academic success of these schools included intellectually challenging and clearly focused teaching, good record keeping, parental involvement and the creation of a postive school ethos.

Parental Involvement

The inclusion of parental involvement in Mortimore *et al.*'s (1988) list of key factors underpinning successful primary school teaching comes as no surprise given all the evidence we have for the importance of parents in fostering their children's early development and education. In the next chapter we discuss the value of pre-school and early school intervention projects designed to sharpen the awareness of (lower) working-class parents that they have much to contribute to their children's education and to develop their skills in doing so. The success of such projects can be measured in terms of the level of educational skills which children have acquired by the time of their entry into Key Stage 1 of the National Curriculum, including their attitudes and motivation towards school learning. In addition to such projects, however, there is much that primary schools can do to encourage and develop active partnerships with the parents, including those from socially disadvantaged backgrounds (Wolfendale, 1987).

By far the main thrust of schemes to encourage the active involvement of parents in their children's education has been in the area of reading and language, following the pioneering Haringey Reading Project which was centred on a number of infant schools serving lower working-class areas (Hewison and Tizard, 1984). In the LEA in which our own study took place some of the primary schools had been participating in a county-wide programme designed to enhance the role of parents in helping to develop their children's reading and language skills. This scheme, entitled Children and Parents Enjoy Reading (CAPER) has achieved considerable success in the judgment of its authors (Branston and Provis, 1986) and has its counterpart in other schemes operating throughout England and Wales.

In Chapter 2 we described the findings of our enquiry into the partnership links between our sample schools and their parents. Not surprisingly, all schools claimed that they encouraged their parents to help in the education of their children at home but our data do not allow us to judge the strength or quality of the schools' parental links, although there is likely to be some variation in these respects between the schools. A few class teachers from disadvantaged area schools referred to the problems they encountered in trying to encourage parental involvement in reading, such as the non-return of books loaned by the school to the parents, and some teachers described the level of parental response to their efforts as poor.

No one can deny that the challenges facing schools serving predominantly socially disadvantaged areas in their efforts to engage the active support of their parents are considerably greater than in schools serving more favoured areas. Acknowledging this it is vital that the staffs in such schools should be united in their efforts through the development of whole school policies, and should try to maintain a steady expectation of a positive outcome despite setbacks and discouragement. At the same time they will need adequate levels of staffing and resources to meet the challenges they face, a fact that was recognized in the now defunct practice by LEAs of designating selected schools as social priority area schools and funding them more generously. Also it must be recognized that the role of the school in combating the multiple problems of deprivation which characterize such areas is necessarily limited. Their main task is to try to ensure the optimum development, academically and socially, of their pupils, within the framework of the National Curriculum. More than that should not be expected.

In our enquiry we also asked the schools whether, in addition to encouraging parents to be actively involved in their children's education at home, they involved them directly in the work of the school, within the classroom or elsewhere. As reported in Chapter 2, while over half of the headteachers reported that they did encourage parents to assist directly in the work of the school, the roles that they were asked to play were largely ancillary in nature and provided support of one kind or another for the school's curricular activities, such as helping in the school library or accompanying children on school trips. Only a handful of schools actually encouraged parents to assist directly in teaching activities such as hearing children read or talking to them in the context of other activities.

Given that socially disadvantaged children typically do not experience adequate levels of purposeful talk with adults in learning contexts, the need to maximize their opportunities to engage in such talk in their classrooms is all the greater. While the use of parents to help in instructional contexts can arouse anxieties in teachers about their loss of control of the teaching process, properly managed, parental support in classroom teaching activities can be of real benefit both to pupils and their teachers, for whom parents represent a valuable resource (Tizard *et al.*, 1981; Wolfendale, 1988). Indeed, in the context of adult–child dialogue, the observational studies of Tizard and Hughes (1984) and Wells (1985) show that the educational quality of the conversations between working-class mothers and their young children in domestic contexts can sometimes be higher than that between teachers and their pupils, where the teacher's attention has to be spread over a large group. Similarly the carefully managed use of older pupils, or more capable age mates in the 'peer tutoring' of slower learners in key areas such as reading represents another potential valuable resource for the hard pressed teachers (Topping, 1987).

The Need for a Whole School Policy

If effective parental involvement and other necessary features of good educational provision for slower learning children are to be secured it is essential that they should be built into an agreed whole school policy for teaching pupils with special needs. Indeed it is part of their statutory duties for governing bodies of all maintained schools to draw up and report on the school's policy on special educational needs (DFE/Welsh Office, 1993). This should be designed to inform, guide and coordinate the work of teachers and other staff, parents and governors in their efforts to meet these children's learning and developmental needs. Useful suggestions for the content of such a policy are contained in a publication by the CCW (1992b) which identifies some of the principles and practical considerations which schools should take into account when reviewing their provision for children with special needs. These are presented under the headings of 'Classroom Management' and 'School Management and Organization' respectively. Classroom management covers matters of curriculum planning to meet individual pupil's learning needs, assessment, and the organization of the classroom and its resources to provide full access for these children to the learning tasks of the National Curriculum.

School management and organization deals first with school policy and planning, which includes a policy statement on the way the school caters for children with special needs, and also a statement on how the educational requirements of these children are incorporated into the school's overall development plan. This section of the statement also needs to make clear how priorities are to be decided regarding allocation of the school's resources. Second, the policy should establish clear channels of communication relating to children with special needs, both within the school and between the school, parents, governors and outside agencies. The role of a designated staff coordinator for special needs is clearly very important in this respect.

The remaining subsections of the CCW whole school policy document (1992b) concern staff development, including INSET relating to educational provision for special needs; the involvement of external support services, including special needs support teachers and LEA advisors; community links; and assessment and evaluation at the school level. Surprisingly, educational psychologists are not specifically mentioned in connection with support services although they have a vital role to play at all stages of the processes of identifying, assessing, and providing for children's special educational needs (Wolfendale, 1987). They are also well qualified to assist schools in the development of overall policies for meeting children's special needs and in the evaluation of the effectiveness of those policies in action.

Following the passing of the 1993 Education Act the Department for Education and Science and the Welsh Office have published a draft code of practice on the identification and assessment of special educational needs and draft regulations on assessments and statements (DFE/Welsh Office, 1993). The regulations prescribe the issues to be addressed in a school's special educational needs policy which include:

> Basic information about the school's educational provision, including the name of the school's special educational needs coordinator;

Information about the school's policies for identification, assessment and provision for all pupils with special educational needs, including policy on access to the National Curriculum;

Information about the school's staffing policies, special educational needs in-service training policy, and partnership with outside bodies such as external support agencies, special schools and voluntary organizations.

The draft code also states that the annual report for each school shall include a report containing such information as may be prescribed about the implementation of the governing body's policy for pupils with special educational needs. The importance of the fullest possible liaison between schools and parents is strongly emphasized, together with the need for schools to recognize the unique contribution which parents can make to the assessment and educational provision for their children with special educational needs.

Summary and Conclusions

The teachers in our study expressed serious worries concerning the impact of the National Curriculum upon their slower learning pupils, particularly those from socially disadvantaged home backgrounds. While accepting these children's entitlement to the breadth and balance of the National Curriculum they showed genuine concern that the progress and well being of these pupils, particularly in the basic skills, were being threatened by the pressures engendered by curriculum overload and having to push the children towards specified levels of attainment. The recently announced plan to review the scope and content of the whole curriculum and its associated testing requirements will undoubtedly help to relieve these pressures to the benefit of pupils and teachers alike. However such a development, welcome though it is, will not alone ensure the optimal educational progress of slower learning children. Drawing upon analytical studies of the work of urban primary schools serving disadvantaged catchment areas and also reports from various government-appointed agencies, we have highlighted what we judge to be the crucial features of a high quality educational programme for these children. These are as follows:

- the maintenance of high expectations by teachers of their children's capabilities;
- the provision of focused teaching that is matched to children's curricular needs, as revealed by careful diagnostic assessment;
- the selection of appropriate teaching methods and resources;
- the regular assessment and recording of progress towards particular learning objectives;
- the maximum involvement of parents in the teaching process both at home and in the school;
- the provision of high quality INSET focusing on the differentiation of teaching to meet individual learning needs;
- the provision of adequate levels of staffing and resources.

These features are unlikely to be present in a school's educational provision for its slower learning pupils unless they form part of an agreed whole school policy for pupils with special needs which will inform and guide the work of its staff. This policy should, in turn, be integrated within the wider educational policy of the school if the provision for children's special needs is to have the status and priority that it deserves.

Subject to these considerations, the introduction of the National Curriculum should prove to be positively beneficial in raising the educational attainment of slower learning pupils within the framework of a broad, balanced and relevant curriculum. Some potentially beneficial features of the National Curriculum in this regard have been described by Lewis (1991). These are:

1 a shared curriculum framework which means that, potentially, such children are more likely to be working within mainstream classes alongside peers;
2 a shared curricular language;
3 the National Curriculum should lead to such children

receiving a broad curriculum which incorporates non-core as well as core subjects;
4 the acknowledged importance of assessing children's learning at regular intervals, seeing this as being an integral part of teaching rather than providing merely an 'add-on' measure of the end products of learning.

Finally, it should be acknowledged that the National Curriculum and the Education Reform Act which gave rise to it pose some potential threats to the quality of provision for special educational needs as well as potential benefits. The teachers in our study pinpointed some of these, including undue pressures upon pupils to achieve National Curriculum attainment targets and the likely demoralizing effects on the children and teachers alike if they fail to do so and thereby depress the school's published SAT record. In a recent overview of provision for meeting special needs in the ordinary schools, Hegarty (1993) is critical of the limited attention paid to special educational provision in the ERA and also of the piecemeal way in which the various reforms have been introduced, with further significant changes still to come. Together with the threat to such provision which he regards as inherent in the new climate of open competion between schools, such factors make for uncertainty in the education sector and undermine the ability of schools to plan their provision for children's special needs in the medium and longer term.

In the light of these potential threats it will be essential to continue to monitor the impact of the National Curriculum and other changes stemming from the ERA into the forseeable future. Evidence of any damaging effects upon the education of children with special needs could well be instrumental in persuading the government of the day to take the necessary action to counter these effects and to ensure that these children receive the quality of education that they deserve.

On a more hopeful note there is much that could be done during the early years of children's development, particularly during the pre-school years, to reduce the chances that children from socially disadvantaged backgrounds will enter the stage of statutory schooling destined to be slower learners. Such measures are discussed in the next chapter.

Chapter 11

Educating Children Under Five

Introduction

The term 'early years', in the educational context, refers at its broadest to the age range 0 to 7 or even 8 years (e.g. Early Years Curriculum Group, 1989), with the terms 'pre-school', and 'under-5' being used for children in the 0 to 5 age range. In the context of teacher training the phrase usually refers to the 3 to 7 or 8 age range (DES, 1990b). The fact that, in Britain at least, children enter into the period of statutory schooling at age 5 provides a legal distinction between between the age ranges of 0 to 5 and 5 to 7 or 8 respectively. This distinction, which of course is not necessarily significant in psychological or educational terms, has now been reinforced by the National Curriculum. This starts officially at age 5 (Year 1), although, in practice, 4-year-olds within an infant class composed predominantly of 5-year-olds or even older children are likely to be working closely within its framework.

Many official reports and other publications on education in the early years, such as the HMI report entitled *The Education of Children Under Five* (DES, 1989a), and more recently, the Rumbold Report, *Starting with Quality* (DES, 1990b), concentrate specifically upon this more restricted age range. Certainly the principles underlying early years' education discussed later in this chapter seem to be based upon our knowledge of children's patterns of learning and development during these particular years. Nevertheless, if healthy continuity between the education of children under *and* over 5 is to be achieved, it makes good sense to consider the educational needs of young children across the wider age range. In this chapter however, the discussion will focus upon the education of children under 5, in particular 4 to

5-year-olds in infant classes, since this relates to the context of our study.

Basic Principles of Early Childhood Education

There seems to be widespread agreement as to what the basic principles of early childhood education are. In its document entitled *Under-Fives in School* the Curriculum Council for Wales (CCW, 1991) expounds the following principles for the education of children aged from 3 to 5:

1 The curriculum will contribute to the all-round growth and development of every child.
2 Learning through structured and spontaneous play is the springboard into the curriculum.
3 There will be plenty of active involvement and relevant first-hand experiences in an environment rich with possibilities.
4 Adults concerned with the under-5s have a particular responsibility for their care and safety.
5 The contribution which parents have made and continue to make to their child's education is valued.
6 Equal opportunities are offered to girls and boys, to children with special learning needs and to those from different cultures.

The above principles show appreciable overlap with the following principles put forward by the Early Years Curriculum Group (1989: 3), although the omission of any reference to play is somewhat surprising:

1 Early childhood is valid in itself, and is a part of life, not simply a preparation for work, or for the next stage of education.
2 The whole child is considered to be important — social, emotional, physical, intellectual and moral development are interrelated.
3 Learning is holistic and for the very young child is not compartmentalized under subject headings.

4 Intrinsic motivation is valuable because it results in child-initiated learning.
5 In the early years children learn best through first-hand experience.
6 What children can do, not what they cannot do, is the starting point in children's education.
7 There is potential in all children which emerges powerfully under favourable conditions.
8 The adults and children to whom the child relates are of central importance.
9 The child's education is seen as interaction between the child and the environment, which includes people as well as materials and knowledge.

Some of the above principles could be said to apply to all stages of learning but the reference to child-initiated learning, its holistic nature and the importance of concrete experience apply particularly to this stage. Although not putting it forward as a principle, the Early Years Curriculum Group's document emphasizes the central role of the teacher in ensuring opportunities for supporting and extending children's learning, particularly through their direct interaction with the children.

Such principles as those listed above need to be supported by appropriate theory and research and conceptual analysis if they are not to remain at the level of mere ideology. Whitehead (1993) argues that the imposition of the National Curriculum has provided a great opportunity to debate the nature of the early years' curriculum and advocates what she calls a 'developmental curriculum' which is responsive to ways in which children learn and develop during this phase. Such a curriculum draws widely on research in child development in order to pick out key features of children's early learning. Drawing on the child development literature, the psychologist David Elkind has described three major principles which he claims should underlie the education of 4-year-old children (Elkind, 1989). One of these is that such teaching should be interactive and that, in any instructional context, the teacher should serve as 'matchmaker' between the child and the materials. An effective match depends on the teacher's knowledge of the cognitive demands of the materials and the child's cognitive strengths and weaknesses. Similar ideas have been put forward by Bruner (1966).

Educational Provision for Under-5s

The 1972 White Paper entitled *A Framework for Expansion* (Secretary of State for Education and Science, 1972) recommended that, within the following ten years, nursery education should be provided in Britain for 50 per cent of 3-year-olds and 90 per cent of 4-year-olds. These bold proposals seemed to provide the long awaited recognition by our society, through its government, of the vital importance of early years' education. However, successive governments have failed dramatically to achieve these ambitious targets. Instead of a major expansion in nursery education we have seen the growth of pre-school playgroups and an increase in the number of 4-year-olds being admitted early into infant school reception or other classes. With falling rolls most LEAs now admit children before statutory school age.

Study of the Rumbold Report on the education of 3 and 4-year-old children (DES, 1990) and the HMI report on under-5s (DES, 1989a), reveals that approximately 45 per cent of under-5s in England attended some form of maintained school provision in 1989. Of these approximately 24 per cent of 3 to 4-year-olds attended nursery schools or classes and around 20 per cent of children in this age group (62 per cent of 4-year-olds) attended infant reception classes. Of the remaining population of under-5s it was estimated that between 40 and 60 per cent attended private pre-school playgroups. In Wales there has been a strong tradition of children starting school before 5 and it is estimated that, during 1989–90, 70 per cent of all 3 and 4-year-olds in Wales were attending school either on a full or part time basis. Of the total number, just over 66 per cent of pupils under 5 were full time in primary schools (CCW, 1991).

The above statistics indicate that the majority of our 4-year-olds are not receiving the nursery education recommended in the 1972 White Paper but are being educated in pre-school playgroups or infant classes. In the context of the maintained sector, this raises the question of whether the quality of education provided in infant (reception) classes is comparable in quality to that received by children attending nursery schools or classes. The view of HMI, at least in 1989, was that it was not, as the following quotation indicates:

> The quality of education for children under five is greatly influenced by the type of provision within which it takes place. Taking all factors into account children under five in nursery schools and classes generally receive a broader, better balanced education than those in primary classes. The work is well planned with a suitable emphasis on purposeful play and exploratory activity. Other conditions associated with the more frequent occurrence of better quality education in nursery schools and classes include: a narrower age band of children; better adult/child ratios; accommodation which in the main is purpose built or well adapted to the age group; better material resources; and more teachers experienced in teaching three and four year old children. (DES, 1989a: para. 6)

The report went on to describe the quality of education provided in infant classes for under-5-year-olds as lacking in breadth and balance so that the curriculum was not well matched to the children's educational needs, for example, providing insufficient exploratory or practical work to support the children's developing ideas of language before they start on the more formal work appropriate to later stages of learning. However there were some notable exceptions where the teaching was characterized by well planned activities and the excellent interaction between adults and children was enhanced by effective parental cooperation. Moreover some recent signs of improvement in the quality of education provided for these young children were noted, which were associated with the provision of good curricular guidelines, backed up by good in-service training and good staffing and resources. The report refers to the government's LEA Training Grant Scheme which would help in the provision of suitable training in the teaching of this age group but, regrettably, this has now been discontinued.

The Teaching of 4-Year-Olds in Infant Classes

Classroom based research studies of the education of 4-year-olds in infant classes have, in general , supported the judgments of HMI in their 1989 report regarding its quality (DES, 1989a). Bennett and Kell (1989), for example, found that both the amount and the level of play observed in their sample of classrooms was very limited. Teachers appeared to have low expectations concerning children's play and often used it as a time filler. The play activities provided lacked clear purpose and challenge and the teachers made very little attempt to monitor them or to interact with the children during them. On the basis of her observations of infant classrooms Anning (1991) described the teachers' approach to their children's topic work, creative and play activities, as *'laissez-faire'*. Their non-interventionist stance to these activities contrasted sharply with their direct, heavy involvement in the teaching of the basic skills of reading, writing and number. However their tight control of these particular activities was at odds with their expressed beliefs in progressive, child centred education, which emphasized the importance of children's first-hand practical and play experiences. The role played by the Year 1 teachers in our own study in their children's free play varied along the interventionist to non-interventionist continuum, as described in Chapter 5.

In these and other classroom based studies it has also been found that the children spend up to two-thirds of their time in basic skills activities, which leaves relatively little time for the creative, play based activities which are central to the ideology of early childhood education. Our own study showed that, before the advent of the National Curriculum, it was common for the balance between play based and teacher directed and structured activities in classes for 5-year-olds to shift in the direction of the latter as the school year progressed. This seems to be a perfectly justifiable shift in emphasis provided that the children continue to have opportunities for free play activities that are appropriate to their stage of development. The other studies reported above indicate that the balance between the two types of activity is often very uneven. Indeed, in one observational study of classrooms for 6 to 7-year-olds it was difficult for the observers to record any recognizable play activities at all, for these accounted for only 1 per cent of the school day (Tizard *et al.*, 1988).

In Anning's (1991) view the teachers whose work she observed were experiencing an obvious dilemma in trying to reconcile their direct instructional role in the basic skills with their professed role as indirect nurturers of the spontaneous learning of their young pupils. She argued that in concentrating their work in the area of the basic skills they appeared to be, at least in part, responding to pressures from outside school, including parental pressure. Indeed, well before the introduction of the National Curriculum the need to raise national standards of reading, writing and number has been a long-running theme in the media and in the pronouncements of successive governments. The setting up of the now defunct Assessment of Performance Unit some years ago (1975) was a good illustration of this governmental concern.

Given that the infant school curriculum, even for 4-year-olds, showed a strong academic bias well before the onset of the National Curriculum we need to know whether, as might be predicted, this bias has been exacerbated since. At a broader level we also need to ask how the curriculum for children under 5 should relate to the National Curriculum.

The Impact of the National Curriculum on Under-5s in Infant Classes

The evidence to date concerning the impact of the National Curriculum upon the education of children under 5 in infant classes is extremely sparse and urgently needs strengthening. In our own study (see Chapter 5) up to half of the headteachers felt that the National Curriculum had made little or no impact, at least by 1991, while the remaining headteachers were sharply divided in their evaluation of its impact. It will be recalled that some of our headteachers appeared to welcome the 'firmer structuring' of the curriculum for these children that had resulted, while others were clearly concerned by the increasing formalization of the under-5 curriculum which they felt threatened the fundamental principles of early years' education. The latter, negative view of the impact of the National Curriculum was strongly reinforced by the judgments of a group of infant school teachers attending a research seminar held in conjunction with our research project. Collectively these teachers reported that the National Curriculum was leading to the increasing formalization of the curriculum for this age group, with a greater emphasis now being placed upon children's written work and an increase in the amount of teacher directed work at the expense of the children's opportunities for free play and practically based learning. Also, in mixed-age classes the under-5-year-old children were suffering from the preoccupation of the class teacher with formal National Curriculum assessment, particularly during the summer term. Especially worrying was the comment of one discussion group that the National Curriculum had altered their perception of what constituted 'bona fide work' for these children, that is, activities that they thought were validated by the National Curriculum.

The results from our study suggest that the over-concentration upon the teaching of the basic skills, already prevalent in infant classes containing 4-year-old children, may well have become more pronounced since the introduction of the National Curriculum. This would mean that infant teachers may be exerting even tighter control over these children's classroom activities, despite their avowed belief in the principles of child centred education. This view is supported by the findings of Bennett (1992) which described the work of a small authorities project which had been set up to examine the provision for 4-year-olds in infant schools in the north of England.

The study produced evidence that the teachers' classroom organization and control of their pupils' learning activities had become less flexible than before, with more limited time being allocated for children's self-chosen activities and stronger control over the composition of children's groups in accordance with their age and ability. In ten of the seventeen classes observed the children stayed in teacher-directed groups throughout the day, the time to be spent on various activities was carefully controlled and the children remained in the same groups throughout the day. Despite these trends the teachers in the project rated the development of children's personal qualities such as self-confidence, independence and a sense of achievement and enjoyment from learning as being more important than their language, social and physical development, which in turn was rated as more important than their learning of the basic skills.

Like Anning (1991), Bennett is sensitive to the pressures upon infant school teachers which result in a conflict between their stated policies and their practice.

> As learning objectives become clearly defined and attached to particular activities so the notion of choice and self-directed learning becomes harder to achieve. (Bennett, 1992: 42)

Indeed she goes on to suggest that it may now be asking infant teachers too much to offer a wholly appropriate curriculum for 4-year-olds with all of its demands. These demands now include: establishing a firm parent–school partnership; ensuring continuity between earlier learning experience and that provided from age 5; assessment and record keeping; and working with other professionals, especially within the context of the National Curriculum and the expectations of teacher colleagues and parents.

The Impact of the National Curriculum in Nursery Schools, Classes and Centres

In the context of the present discussion it is important to distinguish, within the maintained sector, between the educational provision for 4-year-old children in infant classes and that in separate nursery schools and classes. As discussed earlier there is evidence that the quality of provision and the levels of staffing, training and resourcing are generally better in nursery schools and classes than in infant classes. Separate nursery schools enjoy complete independence from primary schools and even nursery schools within the latter may be considered to have a distinctive ethos which is further removed from the requirements of the National Curriculum than that which characterizes many infant classes.

The evidence to date concerning the impact of the National Curriculum upon nursery education is just as sparse as that described above for infant classes. The most important study we have been able to find was a survey carried out by Sylva *et al.* (1992) in a sample of local authorities chosen to represent different geographical areas. The pre-school centres within these authorities were chosen to represent the most common forms of state provision for this age group, namely, half day nurseries in the education sector and full day nurseries in the social services sector. The survey, based upon written questionnaires completed by the nursery staff, found that most of the nursery workers believed that many of the attainment targets specified in the National Curriculum could be reached by some pre-school children. They also claimed to be regularly using classroom materials which were relevant to those attainment targets. Sylva *et al.* analysed the National Curriculum core subject attainment targets in terms of their compatibility with play-based nursery education and judged that many of them were compatible with the practice of nursery education, for example, listening attentively and responding to stories and poems (attainment target E1, level 1 (b)). However they were concerned to find that even those targets which they judged to be incompatible because they required formal teaching were regarded by at least one or more of the survey respondents as compatible with their practice.

Within the education sector nurseries the main changes reported were in assessment and record keeping which were more curriculum focused, in line with the headings and structures of the National Curriculum attainment targets, and increased continuity between the nursery (age 3 to 5) and infant (age 5 to 7) phases of children's education. This continuity was being achieved through increased liaison between nursery and infant school staffs and also through joint participation in in-service training courses. Both of these changes were regarded positively by the nursery staff in the survey. However, like their infant class teacher counterparts, they were aware of the potential threat to the traditional, play-based curriculum posed by the introduction of the National Curriculum, coupled with increased parental pressure for 'school-like achievements'. In the spontaneous comments made by the nursery staff during the survey the most cited drawbacks of the National Curriculum were the pressure to achieve placed upon the children, as well as the teachers, and the reduced emphasis upon learning through free play. Despite these fears most of the staff questioned felt that they had taken from the National Curriculum what was compatible with their customary practice and avoided aspects which they thought inappropriate for very young children.

It may be that parental pressure for children to achieve academically is increasing, even within the nursery sector, following the introduction of the National Curriculum. In a pilot project which compared views on educational provision for pre-school children in Belgium and the UK David (1992) reported that, compared with their Belgian counterparts, British parents were moving further from the concept of child development as a natural process and were increasingly seeking to shape their lives, for example, by attaching great importance to the acquisition of reading and writing skills at an early age. David interprets this as a challenge to nursery educators to demonstrate to parents that the informal learning experiences that characterize early childhood education yield real and observable benefits for the children, even though they precede the more formal achievements.

Achieving High Quality Education for the Under 5s

Perhaps the major challenge facing teachers and other adults involved in the education of children under 5 today is to achieve curricular continuity between this phase and Key Stage 1 of the National Curriculum in ways which do not violate the principles of early childhood education stated at the beginning of this chapter. In discussing this and other challenges facing early childhood education Drummond (1989) refers to 'an intellectual hole at the centre of the early years universe', namely the current inability of early years' educators to justify and explain their professional practices with convincing rigour. She argues that there is a need to develop a professional language which will enable early years' teachers to link theory with practice and research findings with their own classroom observations. In a similar vein Anning (1991) argues that early years' teachers have misunderstood and misapplied research findings on child development and learning because they have not critically analysed them from a professional, educational viewpoint. She considers that the teachers' own 'common-sense theories', developed through a critical reflection of what they already know, should provide them with the insights needed for them to address psychological and other theories in a more confident and receptive way. Anning provides a useful account of some of the relevant psychological and other research which bears upon the role of the early years' teacher.

Ways Forward

If early years' teachers, and particularly infant class teachers, are to meet the challenge of achieving high quality education for the under 5s which also links into the National Curriculum at Key Stage 1, they will need considerably more support at both the national and local level than they currently receive. Nationally the fundamental importance of early years' education should be given official recognition through the expansion of integrated education and services for children under 5 and their families (Pugh, 1990, 1992). This expansion should be supported by programmes of in-service training for all those working with this age group. The Rumbold Report (DES, 1990) recommends that, in order to provide properly for under-5s, reception classes should enjoy a more generous staff ratio with staff having received early years' training.

Regarding the curriculum for under-5s it is vital that this should remain distinct from, although clearly related to, the National Curriculum. The National Curriculum Council in its publication entitled *A Framework for the Primary Curriculum* (NCC, 1989a) comments on the inappropriateness of young children under 5 being taught separate subjects but also stresses that their teachers must be aware of what strands of learning underlie the collaborative, manipulative and imaginary play activities in which these children engage. In this way, they argue, the teacher can use the spontaneity and enthusiasm of young children to provide the starting points for further work while at the same time establishing a sense of continuity and progression with the National Curriculum framework. The Rumbold Report similarly warns against the direct downward extension of the National Curriculum into the curriculum for under-5s and urges educators in this sector to guard against pressures to engage in formal teaching directed towards a specific set of attainment targets.

The curriculum document produced by the Early Years Curriculum Group (1989) referred to earlier provides useful practical guidance for teachers in their task of forging links between early years' teaching and the National Curriculum. They emphasize the fundamental need for the teacher to interact with the young child in the context of the child's play activities. This requires that the teacher not only realizes the importance of such interaction in developing the child's understanding and competence, but is aware of the best strategies to use in the given situation. The Rumbold Report lists the following conditions which are necessary if children's play is to be educationally fruitful:

- sensitive, knowledgeable and informed adult involvement and intervention;
- careful planning and organization of play settings in order to provide for extended learning;
- enough time for children to develop their play;
- careful observation of children's activities to facilitate assessment and planning for progression and continuity. (DES, 1990: para. 90)

A number of classroom based research studies have examined the quality of teacher–pupil dialogue in various contexts and in the light of these have made suggestions regarding the most productive conversational strategies for the teacher (Wood, 1980; Wells, 1985). It is also necessary for the teacher to have sufficient resources and classroom management skills to create the necessary time to engage in such interaction at an individual level. In this connection Bennett and Kell (1989) recommend that teachers should make much greater use of small group teaching for instructional purposes since it is impossible to provide fully individualized teaching for each child.

As we have already stated, the teachers of infant classes containing 4-year-old children probably face the greatest challenge in achieving high quality education for the under-5s because of their closer exposure to the demands of the National Curriculum and strong pressures to concentrate their efforts upon teaching the basic skills. The recently announced proposals for a significant slimming down in the content of the National Curriculum, including Key Stage 1 and its associated assessment procedures should help the beleaguered infant teacher considerably, as would the provision of protected non-contact time. However the pressure on them to prepare the ground for their 4-year-old pupils to learn the basic skills of reading, writing and number is unlikely to diminish because of their central place in national priorities. Indeed the interim report by Sir Ron Dearing (NCC, 1993b: sect. 3.20) uncompromisingly states that 'The principal task of the teacher at Key Stage 1 is to ensure that pupils master the basic skills of reading, writing and number'. The same section also indicates that the content of these skills will need to be firmly prescribed. While accepting the great importance of these skills, infant class teachers should resist any pressure from colleagues or parents to teach their 4-year-old pupils these skills directly and formally.

The developments just described will significantly help teachers to raise the standard of educational provision for the under-5s but it will also be necessary for them to tap the considerable potential contribution that parents can make towards the education of their young children. Our own study revealed that, although the schools readily endorsed the policy of encouraging parents to actively help at home in the development of their children's reading and language skills, the direct use of parental assistance within the school was largely confined to assistance in non-core curricular activities. Nursery and infant schools are ideally placed to develop and implement programmes designed to achieve a high level of parental involvement in the development of pre-literacy and other cognitive and linguistic skills in the under-5s within both the home and school settings. Whether such parental involvement can truthfully be called a partnership has been questioned by Pugh (1990). Nevertheless, in the new climate of unprecedented accountability, nursery and primary schools need to face the challenge of engaging in a genuine dialogue with their parents regarding the education of their pupils to the highest level of quality.

There is a strong emphasis in the Rumbold Report on the importance of educators of under-5s working to establish a partnership with parents in the interests of their children, as the following quotation shows:

> What is needed is for educators to be able and willing to explain to parents how the experiences offered to children contribute to their learning, and to describe how their children are progressing. They need to be able to share responsibility with parents. This places considerable demands upon the educators: they need to be ready to spend time on it, and to exercise sensitivity; they also need to have enough confidence to invite parents to share in their children's education. They must ensure that they have the necessary skills to work effectively with parents. (DES, 1990: para. 100)

Early Education for Socially Disadvantaged Children

The need for socially disadvantaged children to receive a high quality early childhood education prior to their entry into the first stage of the National Curriculum is even greater than it is for children from more favoured backgrounds. This is because their educational and play experiences within the home setting will tend to be more limited than those of their more fortunate peers. Not only may they lack early exposure to a range of stimulating play materials, books and toys but, more crucially, they may have insufficient experience of cognitively stimulating interaction with a parent within the context of meaningful joint activities such as story telling. As a result they may fail to develop the basic educational concepts, skills and attitudes towards learning upon which the infant teacher hopes to build (see Cox, 1993, for a fuller discussion of educational disadvantage and educational provision needed to combat it). It was for this reason that the Plowden Report argued that attendance at a nursery school is desirable for most children but especially so for children from deprived backgrounds on account of their need for

> the verbal stimulus, the opportunities for constructive play, a more richly differentiated environment and access to good medical care that good nursery schools can provide. (Central Advisory Council for Education (England), 1967: para. 165).

The Committee recommended that their proposed increase in nursery school provision should begin within the

> educational priority areas and spread outward, with a minimum goal of part-time attendance for all 4 to 5-year-olds living in such areas, with perhaps 50 per cent of these children having full-time places.

As we have seen this recommendation, along with that for an expansion of nursery education generally, has not so far been implemented, although it is fair to point out that most, if not all, local authorities operate a policy of priority admission to their nursery schools and centres for the most socially disadvantaged children.

In Chapter 5 we reported the concern of some of our sample Year 1 class teachers that the pressure exerted by the National Curriculum towards more formal attainments was resulting in reduced opportunities for children's free play. This restriction was proving particularly damaging for the slower learning pupils who needed to play much more than other children in order to develop language and other skills. Such concern was shared by at least one headteacher whose school served a disadvantaged area. He deplored the fact that there was now insufficient time for the school to spend on the children's social skills, constructive play and attitudes to learning. However, as we have already argued, the mere provision of free play time in the nursery or infant class will not in itself meet such children's educational needs. The play opportunities need to be accompanied, wherever appropriate, by stimulating interaction with a teacher of other adult.

An important but so far unresolved issue concerning the early education of socially disadvantaged children is whether the traditional play-based nursery curriculum which characterizes most nursery schools and centres is capable of meeting all of these children's special educational needs. Proponents of the more sharply focused and teacher directed educational programmes that have been specially designed to develop children's cognitive and language skills in particular argue that these should complement the traditional nursery approaches or even replace them for a period. The federally funded pre-school intervention programmes in the USA which started in the early 1960s were aimed particularly at poor lower working-class black children and their families. These came to be known as 'Headstart' programmes and many of them continue to this day with state or federal funding. At first there was much disappointment with the finding that the short term cognitive and other gains recorded by the children taking part in these programmes 'washed out' after a time. However later rigorous analyses of the long term effects of a number of these programmes, selected for the quality of their planning and evaluation yielded much more encouraging results (see Woodhead, 1989, for a summary of these).

On the question of the design of these successful early intervention programmes Woodhead (1989) points out that they varied considerably in the curriculum models followed, and in their instructional or learning methods, ranging from a more traditional play-based nursery programme to more specialized programmes such as the 'High Scope Cognitively Oriented Curriculum' (Hohmann *et al.*, 1979) and the highly teacher-controlled 'Direct Instruction' programme of Bereiter and Engelman (1966). Despite this variation, all of the selected programmes shared certain features which Woodhead argues may have accounted for their success. All were carefully planned and implemented, were designed with the age group in mind and had clear aims. In addition they had low adult–child ratios and engaged the parents actively in their children's learning (see also Cox, 1993).

In Britain a number of studies have demonstrated short or medium term educational gains for children receiving specially designed early intervention programmes targeted on very young socially disadvantaged children (see for example Kellaghan, 1977). Some of these were specially designed to develop particular language and cognitive skills in disadvantaged children on the premise that the traditional nursery school curriculum was too diffuse to meet these children's special educational needs. However it has been found that the benefits associated with such programmes do not necessarily outstrip those which can be achieved through good quality traditional nursery education (Woodhead, 1976; Clark, 1988). Moreover a large scale study of the longer term benefits of pre-school education by Osborn and Milbank (1987) found that *all* forms of such provision were beneficial although the highest cognitive and other gains were recorded by children attending nursery schools or play groups. The lowest gains were found amongst the children attending nursery classes attached to primary schools. It was also found that pre-school education boosted the educational achievement of socially disadvantaged children at least as much as that of children from more favoured backgrounds.

The finding of relatively disappointing gains shown by children attending nursery classes attached to primary schools in Osborn and Milbank's study has attracted attention and discussion (see for example Woodhead, 1989). The authors speculate that this outcome may have been because the staffing levels and the curriculum in such classes were more akin to those in infant classes than to those in the nursery schools and play groups. Woodhead (1989) urges caution against taking this finding at its face value because of the complex nature of the methods of statistical analysis used in the study. He also refers to an observational study by Jowett and Sylva (1986) which found that children who attended a nursery class attached to an infant school showed a higher quality of play and learning behaviour in their infant classes than children who had previously attended a playgroup.

A possible advantage of a specially devised structured intervention programme for disadvantaged children is that it provides a clear curriculum framework and objectives to guide the teacher in her or his interaction with the children receiving it. Another possible benefit is that it ensures that teacher—pupil interaction time is built into the programme and not left to chance. As Woodhead (1976) puts it, traditional informal methods of nursery/

infant teaching require a very high degree of organizational skill on the part of the teacher if they are to meet the varying needs of individual children within the class. Their success depends on

> the ability of the teacher to maintain implicitly in the quality of her [sic] organisation of activities and interaction with children the structure, sequence and control which is maintained explicitly in a formal programme (Woodhead, 1976: 74)

The main disadvantage of such programmes lies in their separation from the normal curriculum and this may be one of the reasons why in general British nursery and infant teachers do not take kindly to them (see, for example, Quigley, 1971). Another possible reason for this resistance is the rather prescriptive nature of some programmes, although this can be exaggerated. With such considerations in mind the developers of some intervention programmes for disadvantaged children have tried to develop programmes which can more readily be incorporated into the traditional pattern of classroom organization and curriculum of the nursery or infant class. A good example of such a programme is that devised by Curtis and Blatchford (1981) for disadvantaged children which is based upon the broad curriculum theme of 'My World'. At the end of the day the choice as to whether to use a special programme for disadvantaged, or indeed any, young children must be left to the teacher in the light of her or his knowledge of the children's needs and capabilities as well as her or his own professional style and inclinations.

As we have stressed earlier in this chapter, a high quality early years' education needs the active support and involvement of parents, all the more so in the case of socially disadvantaged children. Nursery schools and units provide an ideal base for the encouragement and guidance of such involvement and the literature contains helpful accounts of successful intervention projects designed to achieve this (for example, Donachy, 1979; Hirst and Hannon, 1990). In the LEA from which our study schools were drawn a school based programme aimed at achieving the active participation of parents in the development of their children's

Educating Children Under Five

reading and language skills was well established in many primary schools and this was extended to some nursery schools or classes (Branston and Provis, 1986). A useful source book for nursery and infant teachers wishing to involve parents more actively in their young children's education has been provided by Tizard *et al.* (1981).

Prominent writers on the needs of children under 5 such as Gillian Pugh (1990) often emphasize the need for an integrated service for children and their families which combines educational, social, health and other forms of provision. One way of achieving integrated service provision is through combined centres, which were advocated in the Plowden Report. A number of these have been developed in recent years (for an assessment by HMI of combined provision for under-5s see DES, 1989b). An interesting feature of one such centre in Scotland, described by Watt (1988), is that it was set up as part of a wider project in which a comprehensive school, designated as a community school, sought to develop its role in an area of multiple deprivation.

In her evaluation report on the work of this Scottish combined centre, Watt discusses the possibility that the way in which pre-school education helps children and adults to cope with stress and to enhance their motivation and self-concepts might turn out to be one of the most fundamental contributions it can make in support of disadvantaged children and their families. This contribution, she suggests, even more than the development of children's language and cognitive skills, may be the main reason for the long term beneficial effects of the early intervention projects described earlier in this chapter. The aim of developing in children what Bronfenbrenner (1979) calls the capacity to be 'self-directing' — to take one's own decisions and live one's own life — is certainly in tune with the expressed aims of early years' educators. It is also a worthy aim for all those who work with the parents of socially disadvantaged children since their self-concepts and capacity for self-directed action may also need development. As Watt (1988: 98) puts it:

> pre-school education even of the traditional 'best' kind can only be effective if it takes account of: opportunities for 'self-direction' in both children and mothers; links with

other pre-school and community agencies; the total context in which young families lead their lives; the next educational stage to which children with their parents will progress.

In this quotation Watt encapsulates the essential features of the high quality early years' education which we have discussed in this chapter.

Appendix 1

The Teachers' Attitude Scale

VIEWS OF THE NATIONAL CURRICULUM

Please tick appropriate column

	Strongly agree	Agree	Uncertain	Disagree	Strongly disagree	
1 We will find the NC helpful because it tells us what to teach and when.						1
2 The NC poses a serious threat to cross-curricular (project) work because of its subject emphasis.						2
3 The NC will force teachers to concentrate on teaching those skills/attitudes that are most easily measured at the expense of those that are less easy to assess.						3
4 I welcome the fact that the NC still allows us to decide *how* to achieve its aims.						4
5 The reporting of pupils' performance will mean that teachers will not be able to get away with poor teaching.						5
6 The NC will seriously deprive the class teacher of professional freedom and scope for initiative.						6
7 The formal assessment of children at age 7 will have a narrowing effect on the primary (infant) curriculum.						7
8 The NC assessments will be helpful in backing up our judgments when discussing pupils with parents.						8
9 The NC is broad, balanced and relevant to children's needs.						9
10 The formal assessment of attainment targets at age 7 is too early and educationally unsound.						10
11 The introduction of the NC means that we can concentrate on the basics and forget about the airy fairy subjects that have crept into primary education.						11
12 The standard assessment tasks (SATs) of the NC are essential to back up the teachers' own assessments.						12
13 The introduction of the NC is a backward move educationally.						13
14 The introduction of the NC means that all pupils will get the same breadth and depth of curriculum regardless of which school they attend.						14

Appendix 2

Additional Tables and Figures

The Impact of the National Curriculum

Table A.1 Headteachers' and class teachers' mean attitude scale scores

Year	HT/CT	N	Mean	SD	T Value	P
1989	HT	26	33.04	4.61	1.33	NS
	CT	31	31.13	6.00		
1990	HT	24	30.62	5.24	1.62	NS
	CT	34	28.41	5.06		
1991	HT	21	29.95	6.23	0.40	NS
	CT	31	29.32	5.10		

Key
HT: headteachers
CT: class teachers
NS: not significant
N: number
SD: standard deviation
P: probability

Table A.2 Teachers' mean attitude scale scores over three years: Headteachers and class teachers combined

1989 (N=57)		1990 (N=58)		1991 (N=52)	
Mean	SD	Mean	SD	Mean	SD
32.00	5.45	29.33	5.20	29.58	5.53

T values:
1989 vs 1990 T = 2.69, p<.01
1989 vs 1991 T = 2.30, p<.05
1990 vs 1991 T = 0.24, not significant

Appendix 2

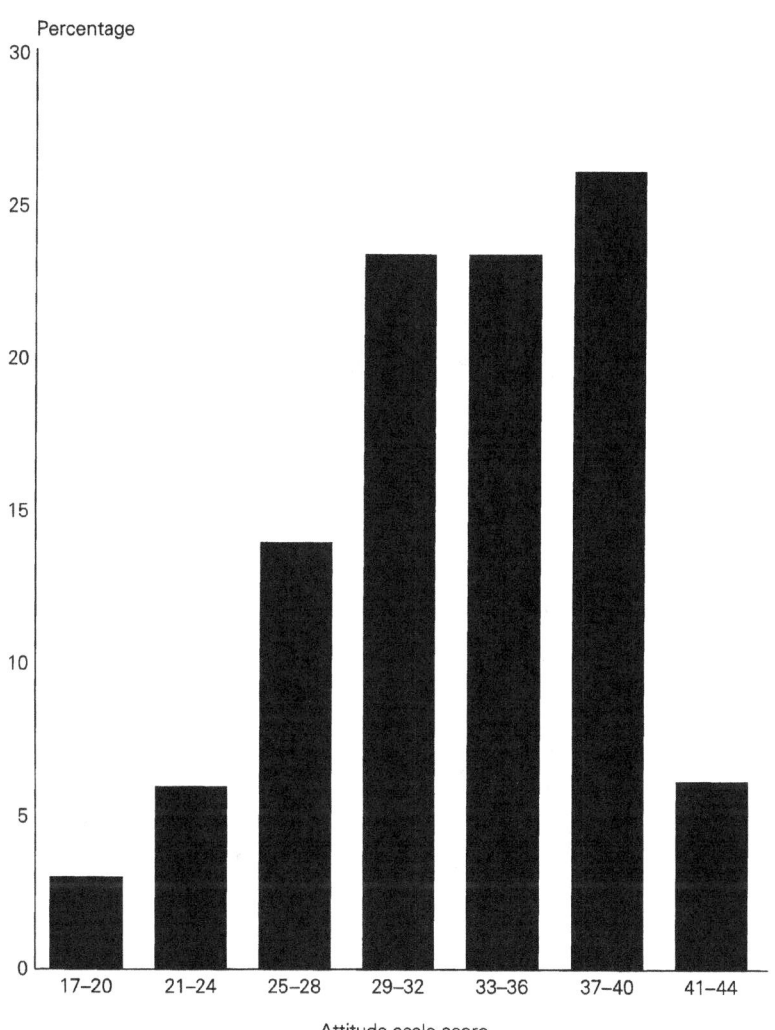

Figure A.1 'Core sample' teachers' attitude scale scores in 1989
Note: N = 35; Mean = 32.77

The Impact of the National Curriculum

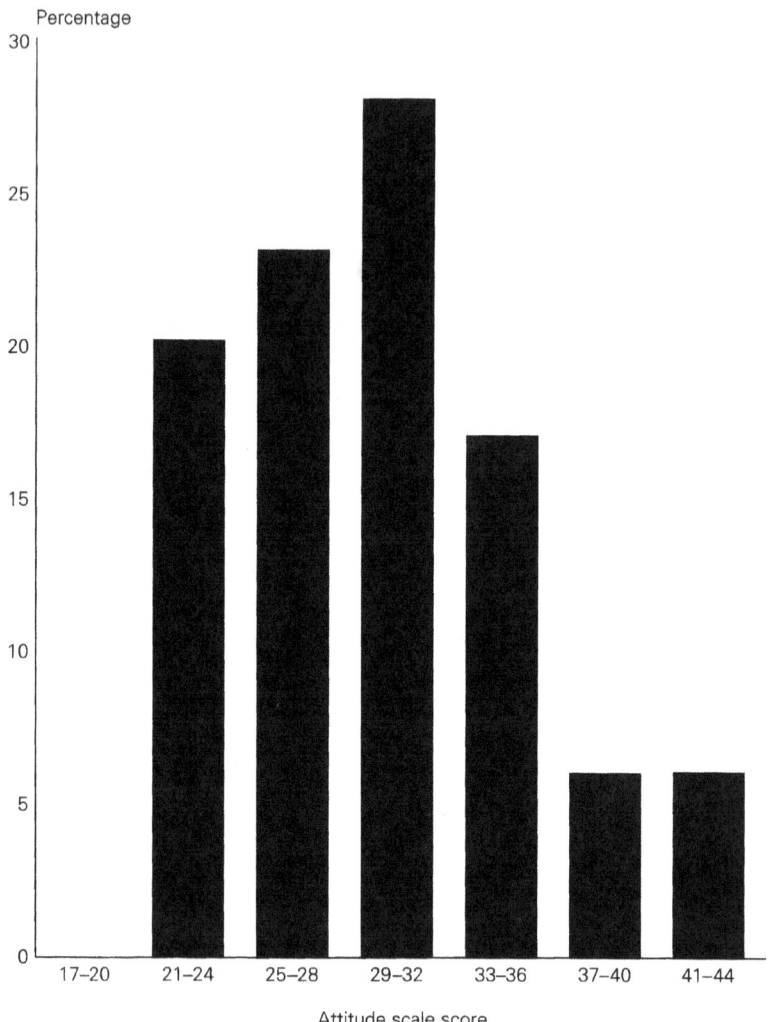

Figure A.2 'Core sample' teachers' attitude scale scores in 1990
Note: N = 35; Mean = 29.80

Appendix 2

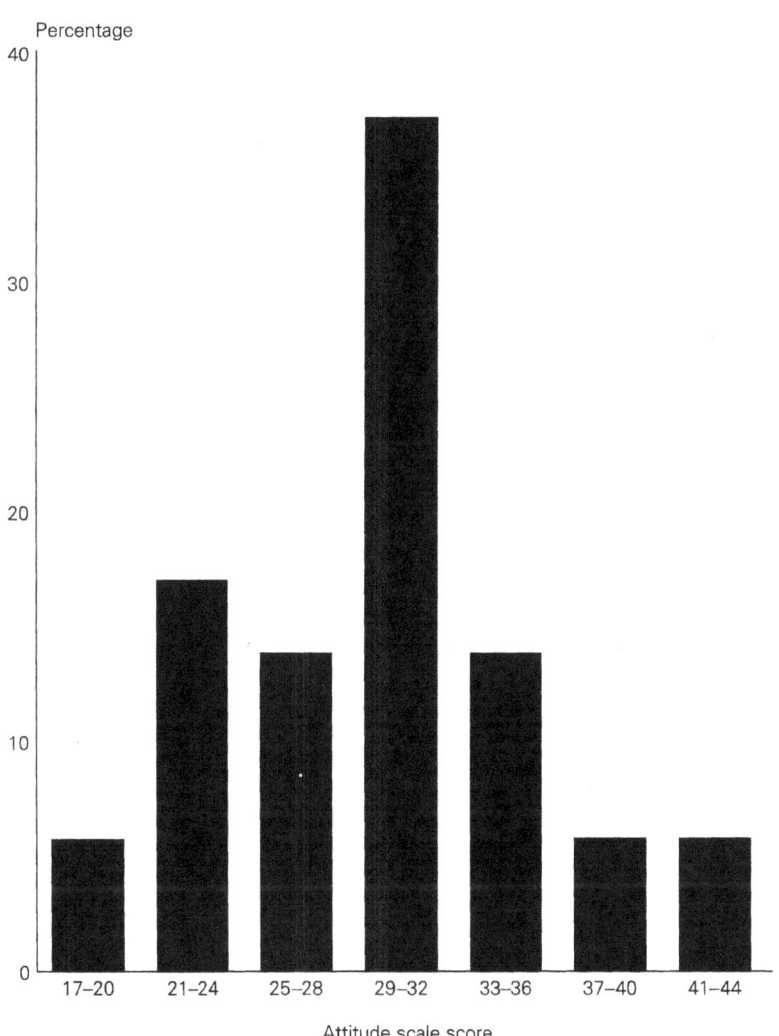

Figure A.3 'Core sample' teachers' attitude scale scores in 1991
Note: N = 35; Mean = 29.68

References

ALEXANDER, R. (1991) *Primary Education in Leeds*, Leeds: University of Leeds.

ALEXANDER, R. (1992) *Policy and Practice in Primary Education*, London: Routledge.

ALEXANDER, R., ROSE, J. and WOODHEAD, C. (1992) *Curriculum Organisation and Practice in Primary Schools: A Discussion Paper*, London: HMSO.

ANNING, A. (1991) *The First Years at School: Education 4 to 8*, Milton Keynes: Open University Press.

BARBER, M. and GRAHAM, D. (Eds) (1993) *Sense and Nonsense and the National Curriculum*, London: Falmer Press.

BENNETT, D. (1992) 'Policy and practice in the teaching of four-year-olds', *Early Years*, 13, pp. 40–44.

BENNETT, S.N. and KELL, J. (1989) *A Good Start?: Four-Year-Olds in Infant Schools*, Oxford: Basil Blackwell.

BENNETT, S.N., WRAGG, E.C., CARRÉ, C.G. and CARTER, D.G. (1992) 'A longitudinal study of primary teachers' perceived competence in, and concerns about, National Curriculum implementation', *Research Papers in Education*, 7, pp. 53–78.

BEREITER, C. and ENGELMAN, S. (1966) *Teaching Disadvantaged Children in the Pre-School*, Englewood Cliffs, NJ: Prentice Hall.

BRANSTON, P. and PROVIS, M. (1986) *Children and Parents Enjoy Reading: A Handbook for Teachers*, London: Hodder and Stoughton.

BROADFOOT, P. with ABBOTT, D., CROLL, P., OSBORN, M. and POLLARD, A. (1990) 'Reading the tea leaves: Teachers' reactions to changes in assessment under the National Curriculum', *Working Paper No. 3*, Bristol: PACE.

BROADFOOT, P. and POLLARD, A. with ABBOTT, D., CROLL, P. and

OSBORN, M. (1991a) 'The conduct and effectiveness of primary school assessment', *Working Paper No. 6*, Bristol: PACE.

BROADFOOT, P., ABBOTT, A., CROLL, P., OSBORN, M., POLLARD, A. and TOWLER, L. (1991b) 'Implementing national assessment: Issues for primary teachers', *Cambridge Journal of Education*, 21, pp. 153–68.

BRONFENBRENNER, U. (1979) *The Ecology of Human Development*, Cambridge, MA: Harvard University Press.

BRUNER, J. (1966) *Towards a Theory of Instruction*, Cambridge, MA: Harvard University Press.

CAMPBELL, R.J. and NEILL, S.R.St.J. (1992) *Teacher Time and Curriculum Manageability at Key Stage 1: Third Report of Research into the Use of Teacher Time*, Warwick: University of Warwick.

CENTRAL ADVISORY COUNCIL FOR EDUCATION (ENGLAND) (1967) *Children and their Primary Schools: Vol.1: Report*, (The Plowden Report) London: HMSO.

CHAZAN, M., LAING, F. and DAVIES, D. (1991) *Helping Five to Eight-Year-Olds with Special Educational Needs*, Oxford: Basil Blackwell.

CHITTY, C. (1992) *The Education System Transformed: A Guide to the School Reforms*, Manchester: Baseline Books.

CLARK, M.M. (1988) *Children Under Five*, London: Gordon and Breach.

COCKROFT, W.H. (Chair) (1982) *Mathematics Counts. Report of the Committee of Inquiry into the Teaching of Mathematics in Schools*, London: HMSO.

COX, T. (1982) 'Disadvantaged fifteen-year-olds: Initial findings from a longitudinal study', *Educational Studies*, 8, pp. 1–13.

COX, T. (1993) 'Coping with unhappy children who have educational disadvantages', in VARMA, V. (Ed.) *Coping With Unhappy Children*, London: Cassell.

COX, T. and JONES, G. (1983) *Disadvantaged 11-Year-Olds*, Oxford: Pergamon Press.

COX, T., EVANS, J. and SANDERS, S. (1991) 'How primary school teachers view the National Curriculum in one LEA', *Educational Review*, 43, pp. 273–81.

CROLL, P. and ABBOTT, D. with BROADFOOT, P., OSBORN, M. and

POLLARD, A. (1993) 'Whole school change and the National Curriculum: Headteacher perspectives', paper presented to the British Educational Research Association Conference, Liverpool.
CURRICULUM COUNCIL FOR WALES (CCW) (1989) *A Framework for the Whole Curriculum 5–16 in Wales*, Cardiff: CCW.
CURRICULUM COUNCIL FOR WALES (CCW) (1991) *Under-Fives in School*, Cardiff: CCW.
CURRICULUM COUNCIL FOR WALES (CCW) (1992a) *Aspects of Primary Education in Wales*, Cardiff: CCW.
CURRICULUM COUNCIL FOR WALES (CCW) (1992b) *Developing Whole School Policies for Pupils with Special Educational Needs: Curriculum Bulletin No. 6*, Cardiff: CCW.
CURRICULUM COUNCIL FOR WALES (CCW) (1992c) *A Report on the Primary Education Review in Wales 1992*, unpublished but copies available from Cardiff: CCW.
CURRICULUM COUNCIL FOR WALES (CCW) (1993) *Developing a Curriculum Cymreig*, Cardiff: CCW.
CURTIS, A. and BLATCHFORD, P. (1981) *Meeting the Needs of Socially Handicapped Children*, Windsor: NFER Nelson.
DAUGHERTY, R. (1992) 'The future development of the primary curriculum in Wales', speech given at Llandrindod Wells, Cardiff: CCW.
DAVID, T. (1992) 'What do parents in Belgium and Britain want their children to learn in the early years?', paper read to the XX Congress of the World Organization for Early Childhood Education (OMEP) at Northern Arizona University, Flagstaff, AZ.
DAVIE, R., BUTLER, N.R. and GOLDSTEIN, H. (1972) *From Birth to Seven*, London: Longman.
DEARING, R. (1993a) 'Have your say', *Times Educational Supplement*, September 17, p. 21.
DEARING, R. (1993b) 'Well, what do you think?', *Times Educational Supplement*, September 24, p. 14.
DEARING, R. (1993c) 'Join the law and order debate', *Times Educational Supplement*, October 1, p. 10.
DEARING, R. (1993d) 'Time to search for a Key to Stage 4', *Times Educational Supplement*, October 8, p. 12.

References

DEARING, R. (1993e) 'And now the trickiest problem', *Times Educational Supplement*, October 15, p. 12.

DEPARTMENT FOR EDUCATION (DFE) (1992) *The Implementation of the Curriculum Requirements of the ERA: An Overview by HMI of the Second Year, 1990–91*, London: HMSO.

DEPARTMENT FOR EDUCATION (DFE) (1993) *Draft Circular for the Initial Training of Primary School Teachers: New Criteria for Course Approval*, London: HMSO.

DEPARTMENT FOR EDUCATION (DFE)/Welsh Office (1993) *Draft Code of Practice on the Identification and Assessment of Special Educational Needs. Draft Regulations on Assessments and Statements*, Cardiff: Welsh Office.

DEPARTMENT OF EDUCATION AND SCIENCE (DES) (1978) *Special Educational Needs: Report of the Committee of Enquiry into the Education of Handicapped Children and Young People*, (The Warnock Report) London: HMSO.

DEPARTMENT OF EDUCATION AND SCIENCE (DES) (1985) *The Curriculum from 5 to 16*, London: HMSO.

DEPARTMENT OF EDUCATION AND SCIENCE (DES) (1989a) *Aspects of Primary Education: The Education of Children Under Five: Report by HMI*, London: HMSO.

DEPARTMENT OF EDUCATION AND SCIENCE (DES) (1989b) *From Policy to Practice*, London: DES.

DEPARTMENT OF EDUCATION AND SCIENCE (DES) (1989c) *Combined Provision for the Under Fives: The Contribution of Education: Report by HMI*, London: HMSO.

DEPARTMENT OF EDUCATION AND SCIENCE (DES/HMI) (1990a) *The Implementation of the National Curriculum in Primary Schools. A Survey of 100 Schools*. London: DES.

DEPARTMENT OF EDUCATION AND SCIENCE (DES) (1990b) *Starting with Quality: The Report of the Committee into the Quality of the Educational Experience Offered to 3 and 4-Year-Olds: Chaired by Mrs Angela Rumbold, CBE MP*, (The Rumbold Report) London: HMSO.

DEPARTMENT OF EDUCATION AND SCIENCE (DES) (1991) *In-service Training for the Introduction of the National Curriculum: A Report by HMI*, London: HMSO.

DEPARTMENT OF EDUCATION AND SCIENCE (DES/Welsh Office)

(1988a) *National Curriculum Task Group on Assessment and Testing (TGAT). A Report*, London: DES.
DEPARTMENT OF EDUCATION AND SCIENCE (DES/Welsh Office) (1988b) *National Curriculum Task Group on Assessment and Testing (TGAT): Three Supplementary Reports*, London: DES.
DONACHY, W. (1979) 'Parental participation in pre-school education', in CLARK, M.M. and PHEYNE, W.M. (Eds) *Studies in Pre-School Education*, London: Hodder and Stoughton.
DRUMMOND, M.J. (1989) 'Early years education: Contemporary Challenges', in DESFORGES, C.W. (Ed.) *Early Childhood Education: British Journal of Educational Psychology Monograph Series No. 4*, Edinburgh: Scottish Academic Press.
EARLY YEARS CURRICULUM GROUP (1989) *The early years and the National Curriculum*, Stoke-on-Trent: Trentham Books Ltd.
ELKIND, D. (1989) 'Developmentally appropriate education for 4-year-olds', *Theory into Practice*, 28, pp. 47–52.
GAMMAGE, P. (1992) *The Tension Between Content and Process*, Lecture given at University College Swansea, Department of Education. 19th May 1992, in the series 'Primary Education-Planning for the Future', unpublished.
GIPPS, C. (1988) 'What examinations would mean for primary education', in LAWTON, D. and CHITTY, C. (Eds) *The National Curriculum: Bedford Way Paper No. 33*, London: University of London Institute of Education.
GRAHAM, D. (1993) *A Lesson for Us All: The Making of the National Curriculum*, London: Routledge.
HEGARTY, S. (1993) *Meeting Special Needs in Ordinary Schools: An Overview*, London: Cassell.
HEWISON, J. and TIZARD, B. (1984) 'Parental involvement and reading attainment', *British Journal of Educational Psychology*, 50, pp. 209–15.
HIRST, K. and HANNON, P. (1990) 'An evaluation of a pre-school home teaching project', *Educational Research*, 32, pp. 33–39.
HOHMANN, M., BANET, B. and WEIKART, D.P. (1979) *Young Children in Action*, Ypsilanti, MI: High Scope Press.
JOWETT, S. and SYLVA, K. (1986) 'Does kind of pre-school matter?' *Educational Research*, 28, pp. 21–31.
KELLAGHAN, T. (1977) *The Evaluation of an Intervention Programme for Disadvantaged Children*, Windsor: NFER.

KELLY, A.V. (1990) *The National Curriculum: A Critical Review*, London: Paul Chapman.
LAWTON, D. (Ed.) (1988) *The Education Reform Act: Choice and Control*, London: Hodder and Stoughton.
LEWIS, A. (1991) *Primary Special Needs and the National Curriculum*, London: Routledge.
MADEUS, G.S. (1988) 'The Influence of testing on the curriculum', in TANNER, L. *Critical Issues in the Curriculum*, Chicago: University of Chicago Press.
MORTIMORE, P., SAMMONS, P., STOLL, L., LEWIS, D. and ECOB, R. (1988) *School Matters*, London: Open Books.
NATIONAL CURRICULUM COUNCIL (NCC) (1989a) *Curriculum Guidance 1: A Framework for the Primary Curriculum*, York: NCC.
NATIONAL CURRICULUM COUNCIL (NCC) (1989b) *Curriculum Guidance 2: A Curriculum for All: Special Educational Needs and the National Curriculum*, York: NCC.
NATIONAL CURRICULUM COUNCIL (NCC) (1990) *Curriculum Guidance 3: The Whole Curriculum*, York: NCC.
NATIONAL CURRICULUM COUNCIL (NCC) (1993a) *The National Curriculum at Key Stages 1 and 2: Advice to the Secretary of State for Education*, York: NCC.
NATIONAL CURRICULUM COUNCIL (NCC) (1993b) *The National Curriculum and its Assessment: An Interim Report*, York: NCC.
NATIONAL CURRICULUM COUNCIL (NCC) (1993c) *Special Needs and the National Curriculum: Opportunities and Challenge*, York: NCC.
NATIONAL UNION OF TEACHERS (1993) *Response of the National Union of Teachers to the Proposals of the Secretary of State for the Initial Training of Primary School Teachers*, London, NUT.
OFFICE FOR STANDARDS IN EDUCATION (OFSTED) (1993a) *Curriculum Organisation and Classroom Practice in Primary Schools: A Follow-up Report*, London: DFE Publications Centre.
OFFICE FOR STANDARDS IN EDUCATION (OFSTED) (1993b) *The Training of Primary School Teachers*, London: HMSO.
OPPENHEIM, A.N. (1992) *Questionnaire Design and Attitude Measurement*, 2nd Rev. Edn, London: Pinter Publications.
OSBORN, A.F. and MILBANK, J.E. (1987) *The Effects of Early Education*, Oxford: Clarendon Press.

OSBORN, M. with ABBOTT, D., BROADFOOT, P., POLLARD, A. and CROLL, P. (1993) 'Changes in teachers' professional perspectives', paper presented at the British Educational Research Association Conference, Liverpool.

OSBORN, M. and BROADFOOT, P. (1991) 'The impact of current changes in primary schools on teacher professionalism', paper presented to the American Educational Research Association Conference, Chicago.

OSBORN, M. and POLLARD, A. with ABBOTT, D., BROADFOOT, P. and CROLL, P. (1991) 'Anxiety and paradox: Teachers' initial responses to change under the National Curriculum', *Working Paper No. 3*, Bristol: PACE.

PROCTOR, N. (Ed.) (1990) *The Aims of Primary Education and the National Curriculum*, London: Falmer Press.

PUGH, G. (1990) 'Developing a policy for early childhood education: Challenges and constraints', *Early Child Development and Care*, 58, pp. 3–13.

PUGH, G. (1992) 'An equal start for all our children?' *The Second Times Educational Supplement Greenwich Lecture, 1992*, London: National Children's Bureau, Early Childhood Unit.

QUIGLEY, H. (1971) 'Nursery teachers' reactions to the Peabody Language Development Kit', *British Journal of Educational Psychology*, 41, pp. 155–162.

SCHOOL CURRICULUM AND ASSESSMENT AUTHORITY (1994) *The National Curriculum and Its Assessment: Final Report*, London: School Curriculum and Assessment Authority.

SECRETARY OF STATE FOR EDUCATION AND SCIENCE (1972) *Education: a Framework for Expansion; presented to Parliament by the Secretary of State for Education and Science*, London: HMSO (Cmnd. 5174), December.

SOLITY, J.E. and BULL, S.J. (1987) *Special Needs: Bridging the Curriculum Gap*, Milton Keynes: Open University Press.

SYLVA, K., SIRAJ-BLATCHFORD, I. and JOHNSON, S. (1992) 'The impact of the UK National Curriculum on pre-school practice, Some "top-down" processes at work', *International Journal of Early Childhood*, 24, pp. 41–51.

TIZARD, B. and HUGHES, M. (1984) *Young Children Learning: Talking and Thinking at Home and at School*, London: Fontana.

TIZARD, B., MORTIMORE, J. and BURCHELL, B. (1981) *Involving Parents in Nursery and Infant Schools*, London: Grant McIntyre.

TIZARD, B., BLATCHFORD, P., BURKE J., FARQUAHAR, C. and PLEWIS, I. (1988) *Young Children at School in the Inner City*, London: Lawrence Erlbaum.

TOPPING, K.J. (1987) *The Peer Tutoring Handbook: Promoting Cooperative Learning*, London: Croom Helm.

TYLER, K. (1993) *Curriculum Styles in the Primary School*, Loughborough: Loughborough University Department of Education.

VULLIAMY, G. and WEBB, R. (1993) 'Progressive education and the National Curriculum: Findings from a global education research project', *Educational Review*, 45, pp. 21–41.

WATT, J. (1988) *Evaluation in Action: A Case Study of an Under-fives Centre in Scotland: Occasional Paper No. 3*, The Hague: Bernard Van Leer Foundation.

WEBB, R. (1993) *Eating the Elephant Bit by Bit*, London: ATL Publications.

WEDGE, P. and ESSEN, J. (1982) *Children in Adversity*, London: Pan Books.

WELLS, G. (1985) *Language Learning and Education*, Windsor: NFER Nelson.

WELSH OFFICE (1993) *Draft Circular: The Initial Training of Primary School Teachers: New Criteria for Course Approval*, Cardiff: Welsh Office.

WHITEHEAD, M. (1993) 'National Curriculum: Understanding the background', *Nursery World*, 93, pp. 10–11.

WILLIAMS, M., DAUGHERTY, R.A.D. and BANKS, F. (Eds) (1992) *Continuing the Education Debate*, London: Cassell.

WOLFENDALE, S. (1987) *Primary Schools and Special Needs: Policy, Planning and Provision*, London: Cassell.

WOLFENDALE, S. (1988) 'Parents in the classroom', in THOMAS, G. and FEILER, A. *Planning for Special Needs: A Whole School Approach*, Oxford: Basil Blackwell.

WOOD, D. (1980) *Working with Under Fives*, London: Grant McIntyre.

WOODHEAD, M. (1976) *Intervening in Disadvantage: A Challenge for Nursery Education*, Windsor: NFER.

WOODHEAD, M. (1989) 'Is early education effective?' in DESFORGES,

C.W. (Ed.) *Early Childhood Education: British Journal of Educational Psychology Monograph Series No. 4*, Edinburgh: Scottish Academic Press.

WRAGG, E.C., BENNETT, S.N. and CARRÉ, C.G. (1989) 'Primary Teachers and the National Curriculum', *Research Papers in Education*, 4, pp. 17–37.

Name Index

Alexander, R. 1, 120, 125–6, 129, 135–6, 140–1, 146, 153–4, 157–8
Anning, A. 171, 174, 176
Assessment of Performance Unit (APU), 172

Barber, M. 39, 40
Bennett, D. 173–4
Bennett, S.N. 40, 120, 122, 124, 154, 171, 178
Bereiter, C. 182
Branston, P. 159, 185
Broadfoot, P. 40, 120, 146
Bronfenbrenner, U. 185
Bruner, J. 169
Burkhardt, H. 146

Campbell, R.J. 121–3, 152
Central Advisory Council for Education (England) 181
Chazan, M. 155
Chitty, C. 1
Clark, M.M. 183
Cockroft, W.H. 140
Council for the Accreditation for Teacher Education (CATE) 134
Cox, T. 102, 148, 157, 180, 182
Croll, P. 127
Curriculum Council for Wales (CCW) 4–5, 51, 54–57, 125, 127, 134, 151, 161–2, 167, 169
Curtis, A. 184

Daugherty, R.A. 122, 132–3
David, T. 176
Davie, R. 148, 157

Dearing, R. (Sir) 5, 7, 9, 128, 132, 141, 145, 179
Department for Education (DFE) 123–4, 135, 142, 144, 154
Department for Education (DFE)/ Welsh Office 161, 162
Department of Education and Science (DES) 134, 147, 155, 166, 169, 177–8, 180
Department of Education and Science (DES)/HMI 4, 29, 39, 166, 169–71, 185
Department of Education and Science (DES)/Welsh Office 6
Donachy, W. 184
Drummond, M.J. 176

Early Years Curriculum Group 135–6, 167–8, 178
Elkind, D. 168

Gammage, P. 139
Gipps, C. 139–40
Graham, D. 133, 136–8

Hegarty, S. 165
Hewison, J. 159
Hirst, K. 184
Her Majesty's Inspectorate (HMI) *see under* DES, DFE, OFSTED
Hohmann, M. 182

Jowett, S. 183

Kellaghan, T. 183
Kelly, A.V. 139

203

Lawton, D. 3
Lewis, A. 150, 153, 155, 164

Madeus, G.S. 140
Mortimore, P. 158–9

National Curriculum Council (NCC) 4–5, 7, 9, 49, 122–123, 128, 134, 149–51, 154–5, 177
National Union of Teachers (NUT) 143

Office for Standards in Education (OFSTED) 42, 56–57, 118, 120, 126–8, 142, 151–2, 157–8
Oppenheim, A.N. 15
Osborn, A.F. 183
Osborn, M. 47, 120, 122–5

Proctor, N. 140
Pugh, G. 177, 179, 185

Quigley, H. 184

Sanders, S. 134
School Curriculum and Assessment Authority 9
Secretary of State for Education and Science 169
Solity, J. 155
Sylva, K. 175

Tizard, B. 157, 161, 172, 185
Topping, K. 161
Tyler, K. 137–8, 141

Vulliamy, G. 124

Watt, J. 185
Webb, R. 125, 133–4, 137, 139
Wedge, P. 148
Wells, G. 161
Welsh Office 142–3
Whitehead, M. 168
Williams, M. 2
Wolfendale, S. 159, 161–2
Wood, D. 178
Woodhead, M. 182–4
Wragg, E.C. 119

Subject Index

able learners
  impact of National Curriculum on
    class teachers' views 67–8, 116
    headteachers' views 71–3, 116
assessment-under the National
    Curriculum
  children with special needs and
    153–6
  effects on the primary curriculum
    139–141, 144–6
  standard assessment tasks (SATs)
    5, 29, 40–41, 63, 81, 108,
    122, 149, 152, 156, 165
  teachers' assessment and record
    keeping
    concerns regarding 40, 76, 78,
      81–2, 86, 117, 122–123,
      127–8, 173
    core subjects in 43–5, 49–51
    perceived benefits of 92
Assessment of Performance Unit
    (APU) 172
Assessment and Curriculum
    Authority for Wales 6, 128
Assistant Masters and Mistresses
    Association 121
Association of Teachers and
    Lecturers 133
attitudes 101–2, 103–9, 112–4, 119

basic skills-teaching of 26, 43, 85,
    74–75, 85, 109, 113, 145,
    148, 151–3, 163, 179

children with special educational
    needs
  assessment and recording for
    153–6
  basic skills learning and 151–3
  benefits of National Curriculum
    for 164–5
  coordinator for 21, 162
  draft code of practice for
    (identification and
    assessment) 162–3
  educational psychologists and 162
  exemptions (disapplications) for
    150
  impact of the National
    Curriculum on
    class teachers' views 60, 68–71,
      84–5, 116–7, 148–9
    headteachers' views 73–5, 93,
      116–7
  objectives based teaching for 155
  research sample in 21–2, 24, 147
  suitability of national Curriculum
    for 149–150, 165
  whole school policies for 21, 161–3
Council for the Accreditation of
    Teacher Education (CATE)
    142
Curriculum Council for Wales
    (CCW) 6, 8, 118, 122, 132,
    137, 139, 141

Direct Instruction Programme 182

early years
  definition of 166
  principles of education for 167–9
  see also under-fives

Education Act 1944 1
Education Reform Act (ERA) 1, 3, 7

free play activities
  class teachers' involvement in 61
  class teachers' use of 58–62
  conditions for 178
  impact of National Curriculum on 60–1, 115–6, 173, 181
  links with formal curriculum 60–1
  slower developing children and 59–60

General Certificate in Education (GCSE) 28–9

High Scope Cognitively Orientated Curriculum 182

impact of National curriculum
  University of Wales Study
    aims 14
    attitude scale 102
    INSET programme 29–32, 41
    interview method 14–15, 27
    interview programme 15–18, 27
    LEA curricular policy 1, 8
    research questionnaires 14–18
    sample classes 23–7
    sample schools
      selection of 12–14, 26
      background information on 19–25
      representativeness of 118
    sample teachers 18–19
  see also PACE and Leverhulme Projects
INSET
  cascade model 29
  children with special needs and 154, 162–4
  National Curriculum and
    class teachers' views on 34–7, 39, 117

    headteachers' views on 32–4, 37–8
  LEA programme for 29–32
  teaching under-fives and 177

Key Stage 2 133

Leeds Primary Needs Project 153, 157
Leverhulme Primary Project 119–120, 122–4
Local Management of Schools (LMS) 3, 7, 88–9, 126

Mathematical Association 133
methods of infant classroom organisation 20, 24–25, 27, 90, 115, 161

National Curriculum
  alternatives to 34
  benefits of
    class teachers' views 82–4, 115, 120
    headteachers' views 91–2, 94–6, 99, 115, 120
  disadvantages of
    class teachers' views 84–5, 114–6, 120–1
    headteachers' views 92–4, 97–9
  effects on class teacher's role and methods 79–82, 89–91, 99, 115, 125, 127
  effects on headteacher's role 87–9, 99, 115, 126–7
  initial teacher training and 142–4
  issues in 129
  Key Stage 1 of 6
  manageability of 121, 124
  origins of 2
  revisions to 5–7, 9, 128–9, 132–3
  speed of implementation of 123
  teachers' attitudes to 103–9, 112–4, 119
  Wales in 8

Subject Index

see also assessment under the National Curriculum, impact of the National Curriculum, teaching the National Curriculum
National Curriculum Council (NCC) 6, 118, 137, 139, 141
National Society for the Study of Education 140
Nuffield Mathematics Trust 28
nursery education
see under early years, under-fives

parental involvement
educating under-fives and 179–80, 184–6
research sample schools in 22–3, 159–160
supporting children's learning and 70
see also Children and Parents Enjoy Reading, socially disadvantaged children
Plowden Report 3, 181
pre-school intervention programmes 182–4
Primary Assessment Curriculum and Experience Project (PACE) 46, 119–20, 122–3, 125
Primary Initiatives in Mathematics Project (PRIME) 36, 41

Rumbold Report 166, 169, 177–8

School Curriculum and Assessment Authority 6, 128
School Examination and Assessment Council (SEAC) 6–7
slower learning children
see under children with special needs, socially disadvantaged children
SMILE Project 28

socially disadvantaged children 147–8
adult-child dialogue and 160–2
impact of National Curriculum on 65, 74, 84
teachers' concerns about 156–7
teachers' expectations of 157–8
under-fives and
combined centres for 185–6
educational provision for 164, 180–6
pre-school intervention programmes for 182–4

Task Group on Assessment and Testing (TGAT) 6
teaching the National Curriculum
core subjects (English, mathematics, science) 43–51
non-core subjects 2, 8, 23, 35, 55, 78, 112
Welsh (Core/non-core) 2, 6, 19–20, 23, 35–37, 39, 42–47, 49–52, 57, 69, 148
problems in
class teachers' views 76–9, 114, 124
headteachers' views 86–7, 115
rural schools 87
resource needs for 35–40
thematic (cross-curricular) teaching and 51, 108, 112, 117, 125–6, 128, 134–9
class teachers' views on 52–4, 56–7
headteachers' views on 54, 57
versus single subject teaching 135–9
team teaching 25
Technical and Vocational Education Initiative (TEVI) 29, 134

under-fives
curricular needs of 176–70
educational provision for 169–70

207

social disadvantage and 180–6
teaching of
  four-year-olds in infant classes 171–4
  impact of National Curriculum on 174–6
  class teachers' views 62–3, 116, 173
  headteacher' views 64–6, 116, 172
  parental involvement in 179–80
see also early years

For Product Safety Concerns and Information please contact our EU
representative GPSR@taylorandfrancis.com
Taylor & Francis Verlag GmbH, Kaufingerstraße 24, 80331 München, Germany

www.ingramcontent.com/pod-product-compliance
Lightning Source LLC
Chambersburg PA
CBHW070736230426
43669CB00031B/2421